POWER BI DATA
Transformation
From Data Source to Insights

Kiet Huynh

Table of Contents

CHAPTER I
Introduction to Data Transformation in Power BI

1.1 Understanding Data Transformation and its Importance

Data transformation lies at the heart of effective data analysis and visualization, and in the realm of modern business intelligence, Power BI stands out as a powerful tool for this critical process. In this chapter, we delve into the fundamental concept of data transformation and underscore its paramount significance in the realm of data-driven decision-making.

What is Data Transformation?

Data transformation refers to the process of converting raw, unstructured, or semi-structured data into a structured and usable format for analysis. It involves cleaning, reshaping, and reformatting data to ensure it is consistent, accurate, and ready for exploration. In the context of Power BI, data transformation allows us to mold our data into a shape that best suits our analytical goals.

The Role of Data Transformation in Power BI:

Data transformation is the cornerstone of effective data modeling in Power BI. It bridges the gap between the raw data extracted from various sources and the insights we seek to gain from it. Proper data transformation prepares the groundwork for creating compelling visualizations and meaningful reports. It enables us to extract relevant information, identify trends, and draw actionable conclusions.

Importance of Data Transformation:

1. Data Quality Improvement: Data originating from disparate sources often contains inconsistencies, missing values, or errors. Data transformation processes help address these issues, ensuring data quality and reliability.

2. Data Integration: Organizations deal with data from various sources, such as databases, spreadsheets, APIs, and more. Data transformation harmonizes this diverse data into a unified structure for analysis.

3. Feature Engineering: Data transformation enables the creation of new variables or features derived from existing data. These engineered features can enhance the predictive power of machine learning models.

4. Aggregation and Summarization: Data transformation facilitates aggregation and summarization, enabling us to condense large datasets into manageable insights without losing valuable information.

5. Normalization and Standardization: Data transformation allows for normalization and standardization, ensuring that data is represented consistently and can be compared across different variables.

Getting Started with Data Transformation in Power BI:

Let's explore a simple example of data transformation using Power BI. Imagine you have a dataset containing sales information from various regions. The data might include sales dates, products, quantities, and prices. Before diving into analysis, you might need to:

1. Cleanse Data: Remove duplicates, handle missing values, and correct errors to ensure accuracy.

2. Reformat Data: Convert data types, rename columns for clarity, and organize data for better readability.

3. Aggregate Data: Summarize sales by region, calculate total revenue, and determine average order values.

4. Create Calculated Columns: Compute additional metrics like profit margins or growth rates based on existing data.

By the end of this chapter, you'll have a solid understanding of the significance of data transformation in Power BI and the foundational concepts that underpin this process. You'll be well-equipped to embark on your journey to harness the full potential of your data through effective transformation, setting the stage for impactful insights and informed decision-making.

1.2. Overview of Power BI Data Transformation Tools

In the world of data analysis and visualization, the ability to transform raw data into meaningful insights is paramount. Power BI, Microsoft's flagship business intelligence tool, offers a robust suite of data transformation tools that empower users to shape, clean, and refine their data for optimal analysis. This chapter provides a comprehensive overview of the key data transformation tools within Power BI and offers practical insights into their application.

Data Transformation Tools in Power BI:

1. Power Query Editor: Power Query is a powerful data transformation tool that allows users to connect to various data sources, apply transformations, and shape the data before loading it into Power BI. With a user-friendly interface, Power Query Editor provides a visual experience for data cleansing, filtering, merging, and aggregation. Let's take an example: Imagine you have a dataset containing sales data. You can use Power Query to remove duplicate rows, filter out unnecessary columns, and merge data from different sources into a single coherent dataset.

2. M Code: Behind the scenes, Power Query Editor uses a language called M to define data transformation steps. While the user interface is intuitive, advanced users can directly manipulate data using M code for more intricate transformations. For instance: You can use M code to create custom functions that perform specific data transformations. This might involve parsing complex text data, calculating advanced metrics, or handling conditional logic.

3. DAX (Data Analysis Expressions): DAX is a formula language specifically designed for data analysis and calculations within Power BI. While it is widely known for its use in creating measures for calculations, DAX can also be used for data transformation. Here's an example: Suppose you have a dataset with a date column. You can use DAX to create a new column that calculates the quarter or year based on the date values.

Practical Application:

Let's walk through a step-by-step example of using Power Query Editor to transform data:

1. Connect to Data Source: Open Power BI and click on the "Home" tab. Choose "Get Data" and select your data source, such as an Excel file or a database.

2. Transform Data: Once the data is loaded, the Power Query Editor window opens. Here, you can perform various transformations. Let's say you want to clean a "Name" column by removing unnecessary spaces and converting it to uppercase.

3. Apply Transformations: Select the "Name" column, go to the "Transform" tab, and choose "Replace Values." Specify the space character to replace with no space. Then, go to the "Text" tab and select "UPPERCASE."

4. Close and Load: After applying the transformations, click "Close & Apply" to load the cleaned data into Power BI.

By the end of this chapter, you will have gained a solid understanding of the data transformation tools available in Power BI and how they can be used to shape your data for analysis. You'll be equipped with practical insights into transforming real-world datasets, setting the stage for more advanced techniques covered in subsequent chapters.

1.3. Getting Familiar with Power Query Editor

Power Query Editor is a pivotal component of Power BI that empowers users to efficiently transform and shape data. It provides a comprehensive suite of tools and functionalities for data cleansing, restructuring, and enrichment. In this section, we will delve into the key features of Power Query Editor and explore how to navigate its interface.

Key Features of Power Query Editor:

1. Data Source Connectivity: Power Query Editor supports a wide range of data sources, including databases, Excel files, CSV files, web services, and more. You can easily connect to your data source by clicking on the "Home" tab and selecting "Get Data."

2. Query Preview: Once you connect to a data source, the Power Query Editor window displays a preview of your data. This allows you to assess the structure and content of your data before applying any transformations.

3. Applied Steps: Power Query Editor operates on a step-by-step basis. Each transformation you apply to your data is recorded as an "Applied Step." You can view and modify these steps in the "Query Settings" pane on the right side of the window.

4. Transformation Options: Power Query Editor offers a rich set of transformation options, including filtering, sorting, grouping, merging, pivoting, unpivoting, and more. These options can be accessed through the various tabs in the Power Query Editor ribbon.

5. Formula Bar: The Formula Bar in Power Query Editor allows you to enter and edit transformations using the M formula language. It also provides syntax highlighting and autocompletion for easier formula creation.

Navigating Power Query Editor:

Let's walk through the process of using Power Query Editor to transform data from an Excel file:

1. Connect to Data Source: Open Power BI and click on the "Home" tab. Choose "Get Data" and select "Excel." Browse to your Excel file and select the desired worksheet.

2. Preview Data: Power Query Editor will display a preview of your data. Take a moment to explore the columns and values to understand the structure.

3. Applying Transformations: Suppose you want to filter out rows where the "Sales" column is less than $1,000. Click on the "Sales" column header, go to the "Home" tab, and select "Keep Rows" > "Greater Than or Equal To." Enter the value 1000.

4. Adding a Custom Column: To calculate a new column, go to the "Add Column" tab and choose "Custom Column." Enter a formula like `[Quantity] * [Price]` to calculate the total sales.

5. Rearranging Columns: You can reorder columns by selecting them and using the "Move Columns" options in the "Transform" tab.

6. Loading Data: After applying your transformations, click "Close & Apply" to load the data into Power BI.

By becoming familiar with the Power Query Editor interface and its core features, you'll be well-equipped to perform a wide range of data transformations. Whether you're cleaning messy data, merging datasets, or creating calculated columns, Power Query Editor offers an intuitive and powerful environment to shape your data for analysis. As you progress through this book, you'll dive deeper into advanced techniques and best practices for effective data transformation in Power BI.

CHAPTER II
Connecting to Data Sources

2.1 Importing Data from Various Sources

In Power BI, the ability to import data from various sources is a fundamental aspect that underpins the entire data analysis process. Power BI provides a seamless experience for connecting to a wide range of data sources, including databases, files, online services, and more. In this section, we will explore the process of importing data from different sources into Power BI.

Importing Data from Excel:

1. Connect to Excel Data: Launch Power BI Desktop and click on the "Home" tab. Select "Get Data" and then choose "Excel." Browse to the location of your Excel file and select the appropriate worksheet.

2. Preview and Transform: After connecting to the Excel data, Power BI will display a preview of the data in the Navigator window. Here, you can choose to transform the data by applying various transformations using Power Query Editor.

3. Load Data: Once you've applied the necessary transformations, click on the "Load" button to import the data into Power BI. The data will be available in the "Fields" pane on the right side of the Power BI interface.

Importing Data from Databases:

1. Connect to Database: To import data from a database, go to the "Home" tab in Power BI Desktop and select "Get Data." Choose the type of database you want to connect to (e.g., SQL Server, MySQL, Oracle).

2. Provide Connection Details: Enter the server name, database name, and authentication credentials. You can choose to import data through a direct query or load it into the Power BI model.

3. Query Editor for Database: Similar to the Excel example, the Query Editor will allow you to preview and transform the data before loading it into Power BI.

4. Load Data: After applying transformations, click "Close & Apply" to load the data into Power BI.

Importing Data from Web Services:

1. Connect to Web Service: In Power BI Desktop, select "Get Data" and choose "Web." Enter the URL of the web service's API endpoint.

2. Authentication: Depending on the web service, you may need to provide authentication credentials. Power BI supports various authentication methods, including API keys and OAuth.

3. Transform and Load: After connecting to the web service, you can use Power Query Editor to transform the data. Apply necessary filters, merge queries, or create calculated columns.

4. Load Data: Once transformations are complete, click "Close & Apply" to load the data into Power BI.

Importing Data from Files:

1. Connect to File: Use the "Get Data" option and select the file type you want to import (e.g., CSV, JSON, XML). Browse to the file location.

2. Preview and Transform: Power BI will display a preview of the data. Apply transformations using Power Query Editor if needed.

3. Load Data: After transformations, click "Close & Apply" to import the data into Power BI.

Importing Data from Online Services:

1. Connect to Online Service: In Power BI Desktop, choose "Get Data" and select the relevant online service (e.g., SharePoint Online, Dynamics 365).

2. Provide Credentials: Enter the required credentials to access the online service.

3. Select Data: Choose the specific data you want to import and load into Power BI.

By mastering the process of importing data from various sources, you can ensure that your Power BI reports and dashboards are based on accurate and up-to-date information. Whether your data is stored in Excel spreadsheets, databases, web services, or files, Power BI's robust data connectivity capabilities enable you to seamlessly bring your data into the Power BI ecosystem for analysis and visualization.

2.2. Connecting to Databases and Cloud Services

In the modern data-driven landscape, organizations rely heavily on databases and cloud services to store and manage their data. Power BI provides robust connectivity options to various databases and cloud services, enabling you to seamlessly retrieve and analyze your data. In this section, we will delve into the process of connecting Power BI to databases and cloud services.

Connecting to Databases:

1. Choose Database Type: Launch Power BI Desktop and go to the "Home" tab. Select "Get Data" and choose the type of database you want to connect to, such as SQL Server, MySQL, or Oracle.

2. Provide Connection Details: Enter the necessary connection details, including the server name, database name, and authentication credentials. You can choose to connect using Windows authentication or provide a specific username and password.

3. Query Editor: Once connected, Power BI provides a visual interface to build your database queries using Power Query Editor. You can select tables, columns, apply filters, and perform transformations before loading the data.

4. Load Data: After applying transformations, click the "Load" button to import the data into Power BI. The imported data will be available in the "Fields" pane.

Example: Connecting to SQL Server Database:

Let's say you have a SQL Server database named "SalesDB" with a table named "Orders." Here's how to connect to this database using Power BI:

1. Launch Power BI Desktop.

2. Go to the "Home" tab and select "Get Data."

3. Choose "SQL Server" and enter the server name and authentication details.

4. Select the "SalesDB" database and the "Orders" table.

5. Use the Query Editor to perform transformations if needed.

6. Click "Load" to import the data into Power BI.

Connecting to Cloud Services:

1. Choose Cloud Service: Power BI also allows you to connect to various cloud services, such as Azure SQL Database, Azure Data Lake Storage, SharePoint Online, and more.

2. Provide Credentials: Enter the required credentials to access the cloud service. This may include your Azure account credentials or other authentication methods.

3. Select Data: Choose the specific datasets, files, or resources you want to connect to.

4. Query Editor: As with databases, you can use Power Query Editor to refine and transform the data from the cloud service.

5. Load Data: After transformations, click "Close & Apply" to load the data into Power BI.

Example: Connecting to Azure SQL Database:

Suppose you want to connect Power BI to an Azure SQL Database that contains sales data. Here's how to do it:

1. Open Power BI Desktop.

2. Navigate to the "Home" tab and click "Get Data."

3. Choose "Azure" and then "Azure SQL Database."

4. Enter the server name and database credentials.

5. Select the desired tables or views containing the sales data.

6. Apply transformations using Power Query Editor.

7. Click "Close & Apply" to import the data into Power BI.

By seamlessly connecting to databases and cloud services, Power BI empowers you to create insightful reports and dashboards that are fueled by real-time and relevant data. This capability is essential for organizations seeking to make informed decisions and gain actionable insights from their data assets stored across various databases and cloud platforms.

2.3. Importing Data from Excel, CSV, and Text Files

Power BI offers a seamless way to connect and import data from various file formats, including Excel spreadsheets, CSV (Comma-Separated Values) files, and plain text files. These formats are commonly used to store and exchange data, and Power BI's data transformation capabilities make it easy to extract valuable insights from them. In this section, we will explore how to import data from Excel, CSV, and text files into Power BI.

Importing Data from Excel:

1. Open Power BI Desktop: Launch Power BI Desktop and navigate to the "Home" tab.

2. Get Data: Click on "Get Data" and choose "Excel" from the list of available data sources.

3. Select File: Browse and select the Excel file (with .xlsx extension) that you want to import.

4. Navigator: Power BI will display the Navigator window, showing a preview of the data in the Excel file. Select the sheets or tables you want to import.

5. Transform Data: Click "Transform Data" to open the Power Query Editor. Here, you can perform data cleaning, transformation, and enrichment tasks.

6. Load Data: After making necessary transformations, click "Close & Apply" to import the data into Power BI.

Example: Importing Sales Data from Excel:

Suppose you have an Excel file named "SalesData.xlsx" with sheets named "Sales" and "Products." To import the sales data sheet:

1. Open Power BI Desktop.

2. Go to the "Home" tab and select "Get Data."

3. Choose "Excel" and select the "SalesData.xlsx" file.

4. In the Navigator, select the "Sales" sheet.

5. Transform the data in Power Query Editor if needed.

6. Click "Close & Apply" to load the data.

Importing Data from CSV and Text Files:

1. Open Power BI Desktop: Launch Power BI Desktop and go to the "Home" tab.

2. Get Data: Click on "Get Data" and choose "Text/CSV" from the list of available data sources.

3. Select File: Browse and select the CSV or text file you want to import.

4. Navigator: Power BI will display the Navigator window, allowing you to preview and select the delimiter (for CSV files) and other settings.

5. Transform Data: Click "Transform Data" to open the Power Query Editor. Here, you can clean and transform the data.

6. Load Data: After transformations, click "Close & Apply" to import the data into Power BI.

Example: Importing Customer Data from CSV:

Suppose you have a CSV file named "Customers.csv" containing customer information. To import the data:

1. Open Power BI Desktop.

2. Go to the "Home" tab and select "Get Data."

3. Choose "Text/CSV" and select the "Customers.csv" file.

4. In the Navigator, preview the data and set the delimiter if needed.

5. Perform data transformations in Power Query Editor.

6. Click "Close & Apply" to load the data.

Power BI's capability to connect to Excel, CSV, and text files streamlines the process of extracting insights from various data sources. By importing data from these commonly used formats, you can create meaningful reports and visualizations that empower informed decision-making within your organization.

2.4. Web Data Source Integration

Power BI provides a powerful capability to directly connect and retrieve data from web sources, such as APIs and web pages. This feature allows you to access real-time or regularly updated data from various online platforms and incorporate it into your Power BI reports and dashboards. In this section, we will explore how to integrate web data sources into Power BI.

Connecting to Web APIs:

1. Open Power BI Desktop: Launch Power BI Desktop and navigate to the "Home" tab.

2. Get Data: Click on "Get Data" and select "Web" from the list of available data sources.

3. Web API URL: Enter the URL of the web API you want to connect to. Power BI supports various authentication methods, such as Basic, API key, OAuth, etc.

4. API Parameters: Specify any required parameters or headers for authentication and data retrieval.

5. Transform Data: Power BI will retrieve a preview of the data from the API. You can use the Power Query Editor to transform and shape the data as needed.

6. Load Data: Once you're satisfied with the data transformation, click "Close & Apply" to import the data into Power BI.

Example: Accessing Weather Data from a Web API:

Suppose you want to retrieve weather data from an external weather API. Here's how you can do it:

1. Open Power BI Desktop.

2. Go to the "Home" tab and select "Get Data."

3. Choose "Web" and enter the API URL

(e.g., https://api.openweathermap.org/data/2.5/weather).

4. Specify parameters, such as the API key and city name.

5. Transform the data using Power Query Editor (e.g., converting temperature units).

6. Click "Close & Apply" to load the weather data.

Importing Data from Web Pages:

1. Open Power BI Desktop: Launch Power BI Desktop and navigate to the "Home" tab.

2. Get Data: Click on "Get Data" and select "Web" from the list of available data sources.

3. Web Page URL: Enter the URL of the web page containing the data you want to import.

4. Web Scraping: Power BI allows you to perform web scraping to extract specific elements from the web page. You can select tables, lists, or other HTML elements.

5. Data Transformation: After importing the data, use Power Query Editor to clean and shape it as needed.

6. Load Data: Once transformations are done, click "Close & Apply" to load the web data into Power BI.

Example: Scraping Stock Prices from a Finance Website:

Suppose you want to extract stock prices from a finance website's table. Follow these steps:

1. Open Power BI Desktop.

2. Go to the "Home" tab and select "Get Data."

3. Choose "Web" and enter the URL of the finance website.

4. Use the web scraping feature to select the table containing stock prices.

5. Clean and transform the data in Power Query Editor.

6. Click "Close & Apply" to load the stock price data.

Integrating web data sources into Power BI opens up opportunities to leverage external data for analysis and reporting. Whether you need real-time information from APIs or data from web pages, Power BI's web data source integration empowers you to create insightful and up-to-date visualizations that enhance your decision-making process.

CHAPTER III
Data Cleaning and Preparation

3.1 Understanding Data Quality and Cleanup

Data quality is a critical aspect of any data analysis or visualization project. Clean and well-prepared data is essential for accurate insights and meaningful visualizations in Power BI. This chapter will delve into the importance of data quality and provide a comprehensive guide to cleaning and preparing your data for analysis.

Importance of Data Quality:

Data quality refers to the accuracy, consistency, and reliability of the data you're working with. Poor data quality can lead to incorrect conclusions and faulty visualizations. Before you start analyzing and visualizing data in Power BI, it's crucial to ensure that your data is accurate and reliable.

Identifying Data Quality Issues:

1. Duplicate Records: Duplicate records can skew your analysis. Use Power Query Editor to remove duplicate rows based on specific columns.

2. Missing Values: Missing values can impact your analysis. Power Query Editor allows you to filter out or replace missing values.

3. Inconsistent Data: Inconsistent formatting, spelling variations, or different units of measurement can affect analysis. Standardize data using text functions and transformations.

4. Outliers: Outliers can distort your analysis. Identify and handle outliers appropriately.

Data Cleaning and Preparation Process:

1. Open Power BI Desktop: Launch Power BI Desktop and load your dataset.

2. Identify Data Issues: Use the "Data" view to examine your data for duplicates, missing values, inconsistencies, and outliers.

3. Use Power Query Editor: Navigate to the "Home" tab and click on "Transform data" to open Power Query Editor.

4. Remove Duplicates: In Power Query Editor, select the relevant column(s) and use the "Remove duplicates" option.

5. Handle Missing Values: Use the "Replace values" option to replace missing values with appropriate data or remove rows with missing values.

6. Standardize Data: Use text functions (e.g., UPPER, LOWER) to standardize text data. Use conversion functions to handle different units.

7. Deal with Outliers: Use filtering or transformation techniques to address outliers. You can replace outliers with more reasonable values or exclude them from analysis.

8. Data Type Conversion: Ensure that columns have the correct data types to avoid errors in calculations and visualizations.

Example: Cleaning Sales Data

Suppose you have a sales dataset with duplicate records, missing values, and inconsistent product names. Here's how you can clean the data:

1. Open Power BI Desktop and load the sales dataset.

2. Go to the "Data" view and identify data quality issues.

3. Click "Transform data" to open Power Query Editor.

4. Remove duplicates based on the "Order ID" column.

5. Replace missing values in the "Quantity" column with zeros.

6. Use the "Replace values" option to correct inconsistent product names.

7. Standardize product names using text functions.

8. Transform or exclude outliers in the "Revenue" column.

9. Convert data types if necessary (e.g., date columns).

10. Close & Apply to save the cleaned data.

By following these steps, you'll have a clean and well-prepared dataset ready for analysis and visualization in Power BI.

Conclusion:

Data quality is a foundational step in the data analysis process. Cleaning and preparing your data using Power Query Editor ensures that you're working with accurate and reliable information. Understanding the significance of data quality and mastering the data cleaning techniques in Power BI will empower you to derive meaningful insights and create impactful visualizations.

3.2. Removing Duplicates and Handling Null Values

Ensuring data accuracy and consistency is paramount in any data analysis endeavor. Duplicates and null values can distort your analysis and lead to incorrect insights. In this section, we'll explore how to identify and handle duplicate records and null values using Power Query Editor in Power BI.

Identifying and Removing Duplicates:

Duplicate records can emerge due to various reasons, such as data entry errors or system glitches. Power Query Editor provides a straightforward way to identify and eliminate duplicate rows from your dataset.

Steps:

1. Load Data: Open your dataset in Power BI Desktop.

2. Access Power Query Editor: Navigate to the "Home" tab and click on "Transform data."

3. Remove Duplicates: In Power Query Editor, select the column(s) that you suspect might have duplicates.

4. Remove Duplicates Command: From the "Home" tab, click on "Remove duplicates." The editor will automatically detect and eliminate duplicate rows based on the selected columns, retaining only one instance of each unique record.

Handling Null (Missing) Values:

Null values, also known as missing values, can disrupt your analysis. Power Query Editor provides multiple ways to handle null values, such as replacing them with specific values or removing rows containing null values.

Steps:

1. Load Data: Open your dataset in Power BI Desktop.

2. Access Power Query Editor: Navigate to the "Home" tab and click on "Transform data."

3. Replace Null Values: To replace null values, select the column with null values, then click on "Replace values." Specify the replacement value, such as "N/A" or "0."

4. Filter Out Rows: To remove rows with null values, use the "Filter Rows" option. Choose the column with null values and set the condition to exclude rows where the column is null.

Example: Cleaning Customer Data

Imagine you have a customer database with potential duplicate records and null values in the "Email" column. Here's how you can clean the data:

Removing Duplicates:

1. Open Power BI Desktop and load the customer dataset.

2. Go to the "Data" view and click "Transform data."

3. Select the "Email" column and choose "Remove duplicates" from the "Home" tab.

Handling Null Values:

1. Go back to Power Query Editor and select the "Email" column.

2. Replace null values with "NoEmail@domain.com."

3. Alternatively, use the "Filter Rows" option to exclude rows where the "Email" column is null.

4. Close & Apply to save the cleaned data.

By following these steps, you'll have a cleaner dataset with no duplicate records and appropriately handled null values.

Conclusion:

Effective data cleaning is crucial for accurate analysis in Power BI. Removing duplicates and handling null values using Power Query Editor ensures that your data is consistent and reliable. Mastering these techniques empowers you to work with cleaner datasets, leading to more accurate insights and visualizations.

3.3. Data Type Conversion and Formatting

Data comes in various formats and types, and it's essential to ensure that your data is correctly formatted and converted to the appropriate data types before analysis. In this section, we'll delve into the process of data type conversion and formatting using Power Query Editor in Power BI.

Understanding Data Type Conversion:

Data type conversion involves changing the data type of a column to match its intended use. For example, converting a column with dates stored as text to a date data type enables accurate date-based calculations.

Steps:

1. Load Data: Open your dataset in Power BI Desktop.

2. Access Power Query Editor: Navigate to the "Home" tab and click on "Transform data."

3. Select Column: Choose the column you want to convert to a different data type.

4. Change Data Type Command: From the "Transform" tab, click on "Data Type" and choose the desired data type from the dropdown list.

Formatting Data for Readability:

Formatting involves presenting your data in a user-friendly way, ensuring that it's easily readable and interpretable. You can format numbers, dates, and text to enhance data presentation.

Steps:

1. Load Data: Open your dataset in Power BI Desktop.

2. Access Power Query Editor: Navigate to the "Home" tab and click on "Transform data."

3. Select Column: Choose the column you want to format.

4. Format Command: From the "Transform" tab, click on "Format" and choose the appropriate formatting option, such as currency, percentage, or date format.

Example: Converting and Formatting Sales Data

Let's say you have a sales dataset with a "Revenue" column stored as text and a "Date" column that needs proper formatting. Here's how you can perform data type conversion and formatting:

Data Type Conversion:

1. Open Power BI Desktop and load the sales dataset.

2. Go to the "Data" view and click "Transform data."

3. Select the "Revenue" column, and from the "Transform" tab, choose the "Currency" data type.

4. Click "Close & Apply" to apply the changes.

Formatting Date:

1. Go back to Power Query Editor and select the "Date" column.

2. From the "Transform" tab, click on "Format" and choose the desired date format, such as "MM/DD/YYYY."

3. Click "Close & Apply" to save the formatted data.

By performing data type conversion and formatting, you ensure that your sales data is ready for analysis and presentation. Converting the "Revenue" column to currency data type enables accurate calculations, while formatting the "Date" column enhances data readability.

Conclusion:

Data type conversion and formatting are fundamental steps in data preparation. By converting data to appropriate types and formatting it for readability, you create a solid foundation for accurate analysis and visualization in Power BI. Mastering these techniques enables you to work with cleaner and more presentable data, leading to more effective decision-making.

3.4. Text and Column Manipulation Techniques

In the process of data cleaning and preparation, text and column manipulation play a crucial role. Power Query Editor in Power BI provides a range of powerful tools to help you transform, split, merge, and manipulate text and columns to meet your data analysis needs.

Text Manipulation Techniques:

1. Splitting Columns:

Often, you might need to split a single column into multiple columns based on a delimiter. For example, splitting a "Full Name" column into separate "First Name" and "Last Name" columns.

Steps:

- Load your data into Power BI.

- Open Power Query Editor.

- Select the column you want to split.

- Go to the "Transform" tab and click "Split Column." Choose the delimiter and options for splitting.

2. Merging Columns:

Conversely, you might need to combine multiple columns into one. For instance, merging "City" and "State" columns into a single "Location" column.

Steps:

- Load your data into Power BI.

- Open Power Query Editor.

- Select the columns you want to merge.

- Go to the "Transform" tab and click "Merge Columns." Specify the delimiter and create a new column name.

Column Manipulation Techniques:

1. Conditional Column Creation:

You can create new columns based on conditions applied to existing columns. For example, creating a column that categorizes sales as "High," "Medium," or "Low" based on revenue.

Steps:

- Load your data into Power BI.

- Open Power Query Editor.

- Go to the "Add Column" tab and click "Conditional Column." Define the conditions and resulting values.

2. Column Renaming:

Renaming columns for clarity and consistency is essential. You can easily rename columns in Power Query Editor.

Steps:

- Load your data into Power BI.

- Open Power Query Editor.

- Select the column you want to rename.

- Go to the "Transform" tab and click "Rename."

Example: Manipulating Customer Data

Suppose you have a customer dataset with a "Full Name" column and separate "Address," "City," and "State" columns. You want to split the "Full Name" into "First Name" and "Last Name," and then create a new column for the full address.

Text Manipulation:

1. Open Power BI and load the customer dataset.

2. Go to Power Query Editor and select the "Full Name" column.

3. Click on "Split Column" from the "Transform" tab. Choose the space delimiter to split into "First Name" and "Last Name."

Column Manipulation:

1. Back in Power Query Editor, select the "Address," "City," and "State" columns.

2. Click on "Merge Columns" from the "Transform" tab. Choose a comma delimiter and name the new column "Full Address."

3. Rename the newly created columns as needed.

Conclusion:

Text and column manipulation techniques in Power BI allow you to efficiently clean and prepare your data for analysis. By splitting, merging, and creating new columns based on conditions, you ensure that your data is structured in a way that supports accurate insights and visualizations. Mastering these techniques empowers you to handle complex data transformations and enhance the quality of your analyses.

CHAPTER IV
Advanced Data Transformation with Power Query

4.1 Applying Conditional Logic with Power Query

Power Query in Power BI is a powerful tool that goes beyond simple data transformations. It enables you to apply advanced conditional logic to your data, allowing you to create more complex and customized transformations. Conditional logic involves setting up conditions that determine how data should be transformed based on specified criteria. This chapter will delve into various techniques for applying conditional logic in Power Query.

Understanding Conditional Logic:

Conditional logic involves making decisions based on certain conditions. In the context of data transformation, it means defining rules that determine how data should be transformed based on specific criteria. For example, you might want to categorize products as "High," "Medium," or "Low" based on their sales values.

Applying Conditional Logic in Power Query:

Power Query provides several functions and tools to apply conditional logic to your data transformations. Some of the key techniques include:

1. Adding Conditional Columns:

  You can use the "Add Conditional Column" feature to create new columns based on conditions. For instance, you might want to add a column that categorizes customers as "Preferred" if their total purchases exceed a certain amount.

Steps:

- Load your data into Power BI.

- Open Power Query Editor.

- Go to the "Add Column" tab and select "Conditional Column."

- Define the conditions and values for the new column based on your criteria.

2. Filtering Rows Based on Conditions:

Filtering rows based on conditions helps you focus on specific subsets of your data. For example, you might want to filter out rows with negative sales values.

Steps:

- Load your data into Power BI.

- Open Power Query Editor.

- Use the "Filter Rows" option from the "Home" tab to set up filtering conditions.

3. Using Conditional Functions:

Power Query provides functions like "if-then-else" logic, which can be used within transformation steps. This allows you to perform different actions based on conditions. For instance, you can create a calculated column that applies different tax rates based on the product category.

Steps:

- Load your data into Power BI.

- Open Power Query Editor.

- Use conditional functions like "if-then-else" within transformation steps.

Example: Applying Conditional Logic

Suppose you have a sales dataset with a "Quantity" column and a "Unit Price" column. You want to create a new column called "Revenue Category" based on the total revenue generated by each transaction.

Steps:

1. Open Power BI and load the sales dataset.

2. Go to Power Query Editor and click on the "Add Conditional Column" button.

3. Define the condition: If [Quantity] * [Unit Price] is greater than $1000, then "High Revenue." Otherwise, "Low Revenue."

4. Click "OK" to create the new column.

Conclusion:

Applying conditional logic in Power Query allows you to make more sophisticated data transformations and tailor your data to your specific analysis needs. By adding conditional columns, filtering rows, and using conditional functions, you can transform and prepare your data in ways that go beyond simple data cleaning. This advanced level of data transformation empowers you to extract deeper insights from your data and create more accurate and meaningful visualizations.

4.2. Grouping and Aggregating Data

Grouping and aggregating data are essential techniques in data analysis and reporting. These operations allow you to summarize and analyze data at different levels of granularity. Power Query provides robust capabilities for grouping and aggregating data, enabling you to create insightful reports and visualizations. In this chapter, we will explore various methods to group and aggregate data using Power Query.

Understanding Grouping and Aggregating Data:

Grouping involves categorizing data into subsets based on common values in one or more columns. Aggregating, on the other hand, involves calculating summary values (such as sum, average, count) within each group. For example, you might want to group sales data by product category and then calculate the total revenue for each category.

Grouping and Aggregating Data in Power Query:

Power Query offers several functions and tools for grouping and aggregating data effectively:

1. Group By Feature:

The "Group By" feature in Power Query enables you to group data by one or more columns and apply aggregation functions to each group. You can aggregate data using functions like sum, average, minimum, maximum, count, and more.

Steps:

- Load your data into Power BI.

- Open Power Query Editor.

- Select the columns you want to group by.

- Go to the "Transform" tab and choose "Group By."

- Define the grouping columns and specify the aggregation functions for each column.

2. Aggregating Functions:

Power Query provides a wide range of built-in aggregation functions that you can use when grouping data. These functions include Sum, Average, Min, Max, Count, and more. You can also create custom aggregation functions using the "Group By" feature.

Steps:

- Load your data into Power BI.

- Open Power Query Editor.

- Use the "Group By" feature and select the desired aggregation functions.

3. Advanced Grouping Options:

Power Query allows you to perform advanced grouping operations, such as grouping by calculated columns or using grouping conditions. This flexibility enables you to create more customized groupings based on specific criteria.

Steps:

- Load your data into Power BI.

- Open Power Query Editor.

- Utilize advanced grouping options within the "Group By" feature.

Example: Grouping and Aggregating Sales Data

Suppose you have a sales dataset with columns "Product Category," "Country," and "Revenue." You want to group the data by "Product Category" and "Country" and calculate the total revenue and average revenue for each group.

Steps:

1. Open Power BI and load the sales dataset.

2. Go to Power Query Editor and select the "Product Category" and "Country" columns.

3. Click on the "Group By" button in the "Transform" tab.

4. In the "Group By" dialog, select "Product Category" and "Country" as grouping columns.

5. Choose the aggregation functions: Sum of "Revenue" and Average of "Revenue."

6. Click "OK" to apply the grouping and aggregation.

Conclusion:

Grouping and aggregating data with Power Query provide you with the ability to create meaningful summaries and insights from your raw data. By utilizing the "Group By" feature and aggregation functions, you can quickly and effectively transform your data into a format that is conducive to analysis and visualization. This chapter has introduced you to the essential concepts and techniques of grouping and aggregating data using Power Query, empowering you to extract valuable insights from your datasets.

4.3. Merging and Appending Queries

Merging and appending queries are powerful techniques in Power Query that allow you to combine data from multiple sources or tables into a single dataset. These operations are crucial for creating comprehensive datasets for analysis, reporting, and visualization. In this chapter, we will delve into the process of merging and appending queries using Power Query.

Understanding Merging and Appending Queries:

Merging involves combining two or more queries based on common columns, similar to joining tables in a database. Appending, on the other hand, involves stacking rows from different queries on top of each other. These operations enable you to consolidate data from various sources and tables into a cohesive dataset.

Merging Queries in Power Query:

Power Query provides a straightforward approach to merging queries using the "Merge Queries" feature. This feature lets you merge queries based on matching columns and apply different types of joins, such as inner, left outer, right outer, and full outer.

Steps for Merging Queries:

1. Load your queries into Power Query.

2. Go to the "Home" tab and click on "Merge Queries."

3. Choose the two queries you want to merge.

4. Select the matching columns for the merge.

5. Specify the type of join (inner, left outer, etc.).

6. Customize the merge options as needed.

7. Click "OK" to merge the queries.

Appending Queries in Power Query:

Appending queries involves stacking the rows from one query on top of another. This is useful when you have similar data structures in different sources and want to consolidate them into a single dataset.

Steps for Appending Queries:

1. Load your queries into Power Query.

2. Go to the "Home" tab and click on "Append Queries."

3. Choose the queries you want to append.

4. Arrange the order in which the queries should be appended.

5. Click "OK" to append the queries.

Example: Merging and Appending Sales Data

Suppose you have two sales datasets, one containing "Sales by Region" and another containing "Sales by Product." You want to merge the two datasets based on the "Region" column and append the "Sales by Product" dataset below the merged result.

Steps:

1. Load both datasets into Power BI.

2. Open Power Query Editor and select the "Sales by Region" dataset.

3. Click on "Merge Queries" and choose the "Sales by Product" dataset.

4. Select the "Region" column for merging and choose an inner join.

5. Customize merge options if needed and click "OK."

6. Append the "Sales by Product" dataset to the merged result using the "Append Queries" feature.

7. Arrange the order of appending as needed and click "OK."

Conclusion:

Merging and appending queries are essential techniques in Power Query that enable you to combine data from different sources or tables efficiently. Whether you need to consolidate related data or stack similar datasets, Power Query's "Merge Queries" and "Append Queries" features provide powerful tools for achieving these tasks. This chapter has introduced you to the concepts and steps involved in merging and appending queries, allowing you to harness the full potential of Power Query for your data transformation needs.

4.4. Combining Data from Multiple Sources

In the world of data analysis and reporting, it's common to work with data that originates from various sources, such as databases, spreadsheets, APIs, and web services. Combining data from multiple sources is a critical step in creating comprehensive and meaningful insights. Power Query offers robust tools to efficiently merge and consolidate data from multiple sources, providing a seamless process for data integration.

Understanding Data Combination:

Data combination involves the process of gathering and consolidating information from multiple sources into a single dataset. This process is crucial for creating a unified view of your data, enabling you to perform analyses and generate reports with accuracy.

Combining Data from Multiple Sources in Power Query:

Power Query simplifies the process of combining data from multiple sources by offering intuitive features and functionalities. Whether you're dealing with structured databases, semi-structured files, or web-based data, Power Query provides a consistent approach to integration.

Steps for Combining Data from Multiple Sources:

1. Identify Data Sources: Determine the various sources from which you need to gather data. These sources could include databases, Excel files, CSV files, APIs, web services, and more.

2. Import Data: Use Power Query to import data from each source. This involves connecting to the data source, selecting the necessary tables or files, and loading the data into Power Query.

3. Data Transformation: Apply any necessary data transformation steps to each imported dataset. This could include cleaning, filtering, renaming columns, and converting data types.

4. Create Relationships: If applicable, establish relationships between different datasets using Power Query's relationship management tools.

5. Combine Queries: Utilize Power Query's "Append Queries" feature to stack the rows from different queries on top of each other. Alternatively, use the "Merge Queries" feature to combine data based on common columns.

6. Data Consolidation: Further transform and consolidate the combined data as needed. This could involve additional data cleaning, aggregation, or calculations.

7. Data Load and Refresh: Load the final combined dataset into Power BI or your preferred data analysis tool. Schedule refreshes if your data sources are dynamic.

Example: Combining Sales Data from Different Regions

Suppose you have sales data for different regions stored in separate Excel files. You want to combine the sales data from these files into a single dataset for comprehensive analysis.

Steps:

1. Import data from the Excel files using Power Query.

2. Apply any necessary data transformation steps, such as renaming columns and removing unnecessary columns.

3. Use the "Append Queries" feature to combine the sales data from different regions.

4. Further transform and clean the combined dataset, such as handling null values or standardizing formats.

5. Load the final dataset into Power BI for analysis and reporting.

Conclusion:

Combining data from multiple sources is a fundamental skill in data transformation, and Power Query provides an efficient and user-friendly approach to achieve this. Whether you're dealing with disparate databases, files, or web-based data, Power Query's capabilities for data integration and transformation empower you to create a unified and coherent dataset. This chapter has introduced you to the concept of combining data from multiple sources and outlined the steps to perform this task using Power Query, enabling you to leverage the full potential of your data for insights and decision-making.

CHAPTER V
Data Shaping and Query Folding

5.1 Exploring Data Shaping Concepts

Data shaping is a fundamental aspect of data transformation, enabling you to mold and structure your data into the desired format for analysis and reporting. In Power Query, data shaping involves a series of operations that modify the structure, organization, and presentation of your data. This chapter explores various data shaping concepts and techniques within Power Query, providing you with the knowledge and tools to effectively reshape your data.

Understanding Data Shaping:

Data shaping refers to the process of restructuring, reformatting, and reorganizing your data to make it more suitable for analysis. It involves tasks such as pivoting, unpivoting, transposing, and aggregating data to meet specific analytical requirements.

Common Data Shaping Techniques:

1. Pivoting and Unpivoting: Pivoting involves transforming data from a tall format (multiple rows) into a wide format (fewer rows with more columns). Unpivoting is the reverse process. For example, you might pivot sales data by months to create a summary table with each column representing a month's sales.

2. Transposing Data: Transposing involves flipping rows and columns. This is useful when you want to change the orientation of your data for better analysis. For instance, transposing a table with years in rows and months in columns can provide a month-by-month analysis.

3. Aggregating Data: Aggregating data involves summarizing data based on certain criteria. You can perform aggregation operations like sum, average, count, or maximum to create meaningful insights from your data.

Data Shaping in Power Query:

Power Query provides a wide range of data shaping tools and functions that empower you to reshape your data with ease.

Steps for Data Shaping in Power Query:

1. Import Data: Start by importing your data into Power Query from various sources such as databases, Excel files, or CSV files.

2. Select Data Shaping Transformations: Choose the appropriate data shaping transformations based on your analysis goals. For example, if you want to pivot data, use the "Pivot Column" transformation.

3. Configure Transformations: Configure the selected transformation by specifying the necessary parameters. For example, when pivoting, you need to choose the column to pivot and the values to aggregate.

4. Apply Additional Transformations: Apply any additional data transformations you need, such as filtering, sorting, or renaming columns.

5. Review and Preview: Review the changes you've made in the Power Query editor and preview the transformed data.

6. Load the Data: Once you're satisfied with the data shaping transformations, load the transformed data into Power BI or your chosen analysis tool.

Example: Pivoting Sales Data by Month

Suppose you have sales data with multiple rows for each product and sales month. You want to pivot this data to analyze total sales for each product by month.

Steps:

1. Import the sales data into Power Query.

2. Select the sales month column and choose the "Pivot Column" transformation.

3. Configure the pivot transformation by choosing the sales month as the column to pivot and selecting the aggregation function (e.g., sum).

4. Apply any additional transformations, such as renaming columns or filtering data.

5. Load the transformed data into Power BI for further analysis.

Conclusion:

Data shaping is a crucial skill in data transformation, allowing you to reshape your data to fit your analytical needs. Power Query provides an array of tools to perform data shaping tasks efficiently. This chapter has introduced you to key data shaping concepts and demonstrated how to perform common data shaping techniques using Power Query. By mastering data shaping, you'll be able to prepare your data for in-depth analysis and generate valuable insights.

5.2. Leveraging Query Folding for Improved Performance

Query folding is a powerful technique in Power Query that enhances the performance of your data transformation processes by optimizing the queries sent to the data source. When query folding is enabled, Power Query generates efficient native queries that are executed by the data source, reducing the amount of data transferred and processed locally. This results in significant performance improvements, especially when working with large datasets. This chapter explores the concept of query folding and provides practical guidance on how to leverage it for improved performance in your data shaping tasks.

Understanding Query Folding:

Query folding is the process of translating Power Query transformations into native query language specific to the data source. Instead of bringing all the data to Power Query and processing it locally, query folding pushes the heavy lifting back to the data source, taking advantage of its optimization capabilities. This leads to faster execution times and reduced memory usage.

Benefits of Query Folding:

1. Performance: Query folding improves performance by minimizing the amount of data transferred and processed locally. This is particularly beneficial when dealing with large datasets.

2. Resource Efficiency: By offloading processing to the data source, query folding reduces the memory and processing power required on the client side.

3. Consistency: Query folding ensures that the same logic is applied to data transformation, both locally and on the data source, leading to consistent results.

Leveraging Query Folding in Power Query:

Steps to Enable Query Folding:

1. Choose a Suitable Data Source: Query folding works best with supported data sources such as databases (e.g., SQL Server, Oracle) and certain cloud services.

2. Apply Query Folding-Compatible Transformations: Not all transformations support query folding. Focus on using transformations that are known to fold well, such as filtering, sorting, and grouping.

3. Monitor Query Folding: Power Query provides indicators to show whether a query has been folded or not. Pay attention to these indicators to ensure effective folding.

Example: Leveraging Query Folding

Suppose you have a large dataset containing sales transactions. You want to aggregate sales by product category and calculate the total sales for each category.

Steps:

1. Import the sales data into Power Query.

2. Apply a filter to include only the relevant columns and rows.

3. Group the data by product category and use the "Group" transformation.

4. Apply the aggregation function to calculate the total sales for each category.

5. Load the data and monitor the query folding indicators.

Benefits of Query Folding in this Example:

By applying filter and grouping transformations that fold well, the actual aggregation is performed at the data source. Only the summarized results are returned to Power Query, reducing the amount of data transferred and processed locally.

Conclusion:

Query folding is a key technique for optimizing data transformation performance in Power Query. By enabling query folding and using compatible transformations, you can significantly enhance the efficiency of your data shaping tasks, particularly when dealing with large datasets. This chapter has provided an overview of query folding, explained its benefits, and demonstrated how to leverage it to achieve improved performance in your data transformation processes.

5.3. Creating Custom Functions and Parameters

In Power Query, creating custom functions and parameters provides a powerful way to modularize and reuse data transformation logic. This allows you to build flexible and dynamic data transformation workflows. In this section, we'll explore the process of creating custom functions and parameters in Power Query, along with examples to illustrate their practical applications.

Understanding Custom Functions:

A custom function is a user-defined operation that encapsulates a set of Power Query transformations. By creating custom functions, you can package a sequence of transformation steps into a single reusable unit, making your data transformation process more organized and efficient.

Creating Custom Functions:

Step 1: Define the Function

1. Open Power Query Editor.

2. Go to the "Home" tab and click on "New Source."

3. Choose "Blank Query" to start building your custom function.

Step 2: Define Parameters

1. Use the "let" expression to define parameters that will be used in your function. For example:

```
```

let

    Source = (param1, param2) => ...

in

    Source
```
```

Step 3: Implement Transformations

1. Inside the function, use the parameters to build your data transformation logic. For instance:

```
```

let

   Source = (param1, param2) =>

      let

         ...

      in

         ...

in

   Source
```
```

Step 4: Invoke the Function

1. To use the custom function, invoke it with specific arguments. For example:

```
```

let

   Result = Source(arg1, arg2)

in

   Result
```
```

Practical Example: Creating a Custom Function

Suppose you have a dataset containing sales data, and you often need to calculate the total sales amount. Instead of repeating the same aggregation steps, you can create a custom function.

Steps:

1. Open Power Query Editor.

2. Go to the "Home" tab and click on "New Source."

3. Choose "Blank Query" and define parameters:

```
    ```

  let

    GetTotalSales = (data) =>

      let

        TotalSales = Table.Group(data, {"Product"}, {{"TotalSales", each List.Sum([Sales]), type number}})

      in

        TotalSales

  in

    GetTotalSales

    ```
```

4. Invoke the function with your dataset:

```
    ```

  let

    Source = GetTotalSales(yourSalesData)

  in

    Source

    ```
```

Understanding Parameters:

Parameters allow you to make your custom functions more flexible. Instead of hardcoding values, you can pass inputs to the function, making it adaptable to different scenarios.

Creating Parameters:

Step 1: Define Parameters

1. Open Power Query Editor.

2. Go to the "View" tab and enable the "Advanced Editor."

3. Define parameters using the "let" expression:

```
let
    param1 = value1,
    param2 = value2
in
    ...
```

Step 2: Use Parameters

1. Inside the function, use the defined parameters as needed:

```
let
    Source = ...
in
```

Source

```
```

Practical Example: Using Parameters

Continuing from the previous example, let's add a parameter for the sales threshold. This parameter allows you to filter out low-sales products.

Steps:

1. Open Power Query Editor.

2. Define a parameter for the sales threshold:

```
let

    salesThreshold = 1000

in

    ...
```

3. Inside the function, use the parameter to filter products based on the sales threshold:

```
let

    Source = Table.SelectRows(data, each [Sales] >= salesThreshold)

in

    Source
```

```
```

Conclusion:

Creating custom functions and parameters in Power Query empowers you to encapsulate and reuse complex data transformation logic. This enhances the efficiency and modularity of your data shaping tasks. By following the steps and examples provided in this chapter, you can harness the full potential of custom functions and parameters to streamline your data transformation workflows.

CHAPTER VI
Transforming Complex Data Structures

6.1 Working with Hierarchical and Nested Data

As data becomes more complex, it often involves hierarchical or nested structures, such as JSON arrays or XML files. Power Query provides robust tools to handle such data, enabling you to transform and flatten hierarchical structures for analysis. In this chapter, we'll delve into techniques for working with hierarchical and nested data using Power Query.

Understanding Hierarchical and Nested Data:

Hierarchical data involves organizing information into levels of parent-child relationships. Nested data structures include arrays or records within records. Dealing with such data requires extracting, flattening, and transforming it to gain insights effectively.

Working with Hierarchical Data:

Step 1: Import the Data

1. Open Power Query Editor.

2. Connect to your data source containing hierarchical data, such as a JSON file.

3. Load the data into Power Query.

Step 2: Expand Columns

1. Locate the column containing hierarchical data.

2. Right-click the column header and select "Expand" to view the nested elements.

Step 3: Transform Data

1. Apply transformations to the expanded data as needed. For example, filter, group, or aggregate data within the hierarchy.

Working with Nested Data:

Step 1: Import the Data

1. Connect to your data source containing nested data, like JSON arrays or XML files.

2. Load the data into Power Query.

Step 2: Expand Columns

1. Similar to hierarchical data, right-click the column header and select "Expand" to view the nested elements.

Step 3: Transform Data

1. Apply transformations to the nested data. You can filter, reshape, or extract specific information from nested arrays or records.

Practical Example: Working with Hierarchical and Nested Data

Suppose you have a JSON file containing sales data with nested information about products and customers. You want to analyze sales by product category and customer region.

Steps:

1. Import Data:

   - Open Power Query Editor.

   - Connect to the JSON file containing sales data.

   - Load the data into Power Query.

2. Expand Columns:

   - Locate the "Products" and "Customers" columns.

   - Right-click each column header and select "Expand" to reveal nested details.

3. Transform Data:

   - Filter data as needed, e.g., focus on a specific time period.

   - Group data by product category and customer region.

   - Aggregate sales values within the groups.

4. Create Visualizations:

   - Load the transformed data into Power BI.

   - Create visualizations like bar charts to showcase sales by product category and customer region.

Handling Complex Hierarchies:

Sometimes, data involves intricate hierarchies with multiple levels. You can recursively apply expansion and transformations to navigate and analyze complex structures effectively.

Conclusion:

Working with hierarchical and nested data is a critical skill for data analysts. Power Query simplifies this process by providing intuitive tools for data extraction, transformation, and analysis. By following the steps and examples provided in this chapter, you'll gain the expertise needed to work with complex data structures in Power Query and unlock valuable insights from your data.

6.2. Unpivoting and Pivoting Data

Unpivoting and pivoting data are essential techniques for reshaping and restructuring your dataset, especially when dealing with complex data structures. These methods enable you to convert column headers into rows (unpivoting) or rows into columns (pivoting) to make data more accessible for analysis. In this chapter, we will explore how to perform unpivoting and pivoting using Power Query.

Understanding Unpivoting:

Unpivoting is the process of converting column headers into rows, making the data more compact and suitable for analysis. This is particularly useful when you have data in a wide format, and you want to transform it into a long format.

Step-by-Step Unpivoting:

Step 1: Import the Data

1. Launch Power Query Editor.

2. Load your dataset that contains pivoted data.

Step 2: Unpivot Columns

1. Select the columns you want to unpivot.

2. Go to the "Transform" tab and click "Unpivot Columns."

Step 3: Transform Data

1. Rename columns as needed.

2. Perform additional transformations, such as data type conversion or filtering.

Practical Example: Unpivoting Data

Let's say you have a dataset with quarterly sales data, where each quarter is a separate column. To perform trend analysis, you need to unpivot the data.

Steps:

1. Import Data:

   - Open Power Query Editor.

   - Connect to your dataset with quarterly sales data.

   - Load the data into Power Query.

2. Unpivot Columns:

   - Select the quarterly sales columns (Q1, Q2, Q3, Q4).

   - Go to the "Transform" tab and click "Unpivot Columns."

3. Transform Data:

   - Rename columns to "Quarter" and "Sales."

- Convert the "Quarter" column to a date data type.

- Filter out any unnecessary data.

4. Visualize Trends:

  - Load the transformed data into Power BI.

  - Create visualizations like line charts to analyze sales trends across quarters.

Understanding Pivoting:

Pivoting is the reverse process of unpivoting, where rows are transformed into columns. It's useful when you want to present data in a more structured format for reporting or analysis.

Step-by-Step Pivoting:

Step 1: Import the Data

1. Open Power Query Editor.

2. Load your dataset that contains unpivoted data.

Step 2: Pivot Columns

1. Select the column you want to pivot.

2. Go to the "Transform" tab and click "Pivot Column."

Step 3: Configure Pivot Options

1. Choose the values you want to aggregate (e.g., sum, average).

2. Define the new column headers.

Step 4: Transform Data

1. Rename columns as needed.

2. Perform additional transformations, such as data type conversion or filtering.

Practical Example: Pivoting Data

Suppose you have unpivoted sales data by quarter and want to pivot it back to quarterly format.

Steps:

1. Import Data:

   - Open Power Query Editor.

   - Connect to your unpivoted sales dataset.

   - Load the data into Power Query.

2. Pivot Columns:

   - Select the "Quarter" column.

   - Go to the "Transform" tab and click "Pivot Column."

3. Configure Pivot Options:

   - Choose the aggregation function (e.g., sum) for the sales values.

   - Define the new column headers as Q1, Q2, Q3, Q4.

4. Transform Data:

- Rename columns as needed.

- Convert the quarter columns to appropriate data types.

5. Generate Reports:

- Load the pivoted data into Power BI.

- Create reports with the new pivoted structure.

Conclusion:

Unpivoting and pivoting data are powerful techniques to reshape and structure your data for better analysis and reporting. Power Query simplifies these processes by providing intuitive tools to perform these transformations. By following the steps and practical examples outlined in this chapter, you'll be able to effectively manipulate your data's structure and format using Power Query's unpivoting and pivoting capabilities.

6.3. Handling JSON and XML Data

Dealing with JSON (JavaScript Object Notation) and XML (eXtensible Markup Language) data is common when working with modern APIs and web services. Power Query offers robust tools to handle and transform JSON and XML data into a structured format suitable for analysis. In this chapter, we will delve into the techniques for handling and transforming JSON and XML data using Power Query.

Understanding JSON Data:

JSON is a lightweight data interchange format used to represent structured data. It's commonly used for transmitting data between a server and a web application, making it essential for data analysts and scientists to work with.

Step-by-Step JSON Data Handling:

Step 1: Import JSON Data

1. Launch Power Query Editor.

2. Connect to your data source containing JSON data.

3. Load the data into Power Query.

Step 2: Expand JSON Data

1. Select the JSON column in Power Query.

2. Right-click and choose "Transform" > "JSON" > "JSON column name."

3. In the dialog box, select the properties you want to expand.

Step 3: Transform Data

1. Rename columns as needed.

2. Perform additional transformations, such as data type conversion or filtering.

Practical Example: Handling JSON Data

Suppose you have a dataset with JSON data containing customer information. You want to extract specific fields from the JSON structure.

Steps:

1. Import JSON Data:

   - Open Power Query Editor.

   - Connect to your JSON dataset.

   - Load the data into Power Query.

2. Expand JSON Data:

   - Select the JSON column (e.g., "customerInfo").

   - Right-click and choose "Transform" > "JSON" > "customerInfo."

   - Select the fields you want to expand (e.g., name, email, address).

3. Transform Data:

   - Rename columns as needed.

   - Convert data types if necessary.

4. Data Analysis:

   - Load the transformed data into Power BI.

   - Create visualizations to analyze customer information.

Understanding XML Data:

XML is a markup language used to store and transport data in a human-readable format. Many web services and APIs provide data in XML format, requiring analysts to process and extract relevant information.

Step-by-Step XML Data Handling:

Step 1: Import XML Data

1. Open Power Query Editor.

2. Connect to your XML data source.

3. Load the data into Power Query.

Step 2: Transform XML Data

1. Right-click on the XML column and choose "Transform" > "XML."

2. Use the Power Query Editor to navigate and select the nodes you want to extract.

Step 3: Transform Data

1. Rename columns as needed.

2. Perform additional transformations, such as data type conversion or filtering.

Practical Example: Handling XML Data

Imagine you have an XML dataset with information about products and prices. You want to extract product names and their corresponding prices.

Steps:

1. Import XML Data:

   - Open Power Query Editor.

   - Connect to your XML dataset.

- Load the data into Power Query.

2. Transform XML Data:

  - Right-click on the XML column and choose "Transform" > "XML."

  - Navigate and select the nodes containing product names and prices.

3. Transform Data:

  - Rename columns as needed.

  - Convert data types if required.

4. Data Analysis:

  - Load the transformed data into Power BI.

  - Create reports to visualize product names and prices.

Conclusion:

Power Query's ability to handle and transform JSON and XML data is crucial for data professionals dealing with diverse data sources and formats. By following the steps and practical examples outlined in this chapter, you'll gain the skills to effectively extract, transform, and load JSON and XML data using Power Query, enabling you to seamlessly integrate these data sources into your analysis and reporting workflows.

CHAPTER VII
Time Intelligence and Date Transformations

7.1 Introduction to Time Intelligence Functions

In the world of data analysis, time is often a critical factor. Analyzing data over time can provide valuable insights into trends, patterns, and seasonality. Power BI offers a robust set of time intelligence functions that enable users to perform various calculations and transformations on dates and time-related data. In this chapter, we will explore the fundamentals of time intelligence functions in Power BI and how they can be used to enhance your data analysis.

Understanding Time Intelligence Functions:

Time intelligence functions in Power BI allow you to perform calculations based on date and time values, such as year, quarter, month, week, and more. These functions enable you to compare, aggregate, and analyze data across different time periods dynamically.

Step-by-Step Guide to Time Intelligence Functions:

Step 1: Create a Date Table

1. Open Power BI Desktop.

2. Import or generate a table with date values.

3. Mark the table as a date table by right-clicking on it and selecting "Mark as Date Table."

4. Choose the date column that will serve as the basis for time calculations.

Step 2: Use Time Intelligence Functions

1. Create a new measure by going to the "Modeling" tab and clicking on "New Measure."

2. Start typing the time intelligence function in the formula bar (e.g., YEAR, QUARTER, MONTH).

3. Provide the necessary arguments, such as the date column.

Step 3: Apply Measures in Visualizations

1. Build visualizations on your report canvas.

2. Drag and drop the time intelligence measures into the appropriate fields.

3. Customize the visualization to display data aggregated by the selected time period.

Practical Example: Using Time Intelligence Functions

Suppose you have a sales dataset with a "Date" column, and you want to analyze sales data on a quarterly basis.

Steps:

1. Create a Date Table:

   - Import or generate a table with date values.

   - Mark it as a date table and select the "Date" column.

2. Use Time Intelligence Functions:

   - Create a new measure named "Total Sales Qtr" using the formula:

    ```
    ```

Total Sales Qtr = SUM('Sales'[Amount])

```
```

- Create another measure named "Total Sales Qtr Prev Year" using the formula:

```
```

Total Sales Qtr Prev Year =

CALCULATE([Total Sales Qtr], SAMEPERIODLASTYEAR('Date'[Date]))

```
```

3. Apply Measures in Visualizations:

   - Create a line chart.

   - Place the "Date"[Quarter] field on the Axis and "Total Sales Qtr" and "Total Sales Qtr Prev Year" on the Values.

Conclusion:

Time intelligence functions in Power BI provide a powerful way to analyze and compare data over different time periods. By following the steps and practical example provided in this chapter, you'll gain a solid understanding of how to create date tables, use time intelligence functions, and leverage these functions to perform dynamic calculations on your data. Whether you're analyzing sales trends, seasonality, or any other time-related insights, mastering time intelligence functions will enhance your ability to extract valuable information from your data.

7.2. Creating Date Tables and Relationships

In the realm of data analysis, time-related insights often hinge on having a well-structured date table and establishing the right relationships with other data tables. Power BI empowers users to create date tables and build relationships, enabling seamless time intelligence analysis. In this chapter, we will delve into the importance of date tables and how to establish relationships for effective time-based analysis.

Understanding Date Tables and Relationships:

A date table is a fundamental component in time intelligence analysis. It contains a list of dates along with various attributes like year, quarter, month, week, and more. Establishing relationships between the date table and other data tables in your dataset is crucial to perform meaningful calculations and analysis.

Step-by-Step Guide to Creating Date Tables and Relationships:

Step 1: Create a Date Table

1. Open Power BI Desktop.

2. Import a dataset that contains date-related columns, such as a "Date" or "Order Date" column.

3. Select the "Modeling" tab and click on "New Table."

4. Write a DAX formula to generate the date table. For instance, you can use the following formula to create a basic date table:

```DAX
DateTable = CALENDAR(MIN('Sales'[Date]), MAX('Sales'[Date]))
```

Step 2: Define Date Attributes

1. Enhance the date table by adding columns for year, quarter, month, week, and other relevant attributes. For example:

```DAX
Year = YEAR([Date])

Quarter = QUARTER([Date])

Month = MONTH([Date])

Week = WEEKNUM([Date])
```

Step 3: Establish Relationships

1. Switch to the "Model" view by clicking on the "Model" icon on the left sidebar.

2. Connect the date table to other relevant data tables. For instance, if you have a "Sales" table, establish a relationship between the "Date" column in the date table and the "Order Date" column in the "Sales" table.

Step 4: Configure Relationship Behavior

1. Double-click on the relationship line to open the "Manage Relationships" dialog.

2. Define the relationship behavior, such as cross-filtering and direction, based on your analysis requirements.

Practical Example: Creating a Date Table and Relationships

Suppose you have a sales dataset with a "Sales" table containing an "Order Date" column. You want to create a date table and establish a relationship for time-based analysis.

Steps:

1. Create a Date Table:

- Import the "Sales" dataset.

- Go to the "Modeling" tab, click "New Table," and use the DAX formula to create a date table.

2. Define Date Attributes:

 - Add columns like "Year," "Quarter," "Month," and "Week" to the date table.

3. Establish Relationships:

 - Switch to the "Model" view.

 - Drag the "Date" column from the date table and drop it onto the "Order Date" column in the "Sales" table.

4. Configure Relationship Behavior:

 - Double-click the relationship line, set cross-filtering and direction as needed.

Conclusion:

Creating a date table and establishing relationships are crucial steps in harnessing the power of time intelligence in Power BI. By following the steps outlined in this chapter and practicing with the practical example, you'll gain the ability to seamlessly integrate date-based analysis into your data models. A well-structured date table and carefully defined relationships will enable you to unlock valuable insights and trends from your data that revolve around time.

7.3. Calculating Year-to-Date, Quarter-to-Date, and Other Time Metrics

Time-based metrics, such as Year-to-Date (YTD) and Quarter-to-Date (QTD), are essential for tracking performance and making informed business decisions. Power BI offers powerful tools for calculating these metrics using time intelligence functions. In this chapter, we'll explore how to calculate YTD, QTD, and other time metrics using Power BI's capabilities.

Calculating Year-to-Date (YTD):

Calculating YTD involves summing up values from the beginning of the year up to the selected date. Power BI's time intelligence functions simplify this process.

Step-by-Step Guide to Calculating YTD:

Step 1: Create a Measure for YTD:

1. Open Power BI Desktop.

2. Switch to the "Model" view.

3. Right-click on the date table and choose "New Measure."

4. Write a DAX formula to calculate YTD. For instance:

```DAX
YTD Sales = TOTALYTD(SUM('Sales'[Amount]), 'DateTable'[Date])
```

Calculating Quarter-to-Date (QTD):

Calculating QTD involves summing up values from the beginning of the quarter up to the selected date. Power BI's time intelligence functions streamline this calculation.

Step-by-Step Guide to Calculating QTD:

Step 1: Create a Measure for QTD:

1. Open Power BI Desktop.

2. Switch to the "Model" view.

3. Right-click on the date table and choose "New Measure."

4. Write a DAX formula to calculate QTD. For example:

```DAX
QTD Sales = TOTALQTD(SUM('Sales'[Amount]), 'DateTable'[Date])
```

Calculating Other Time Metrics:

Power BI's time intelligence functions extend to various other time metrics, such as Month-to-Date (MTD), Last Year-to-Date (LYTD), and more.

Step-by-Step Guide to Calculating Other Time Metrics:

Step 1: Create a Measure for the Desired Metric:

1. Open Power BI Desktop.

2. Switch to the "Model" view.

3. Right-click on the date table and choose "New Measure."

4. Write a DAX formula based on the desired time metric. For instance:

```DAX
```

MTD Sales = TOTALMTD(SUM('Sales'[Amount]), 'DateTable'[Date])

```
```

Practical Example: Calculating YTD and QTD

Suppose you have a sales dataset with a "Sales" table containing an "Order Date" column and an existing date table. You want to calculate YTD and QTD sales.

Steps:

1. Calculate YTD Sales:

   - Switch to the "Model" view.

   - Create a new measure named "YTD Sales" with the YTD formula.

2. Calculate QTD Sales:

   - Switch to the "Model" view.

   - Create a new measure named "QTD Sales" with the QTD formula.

Conclusion:

Calculating time-based metrics like YTD and QTD is essential for gaining insights into business performance. With Power BI's time intelligence functions, performing these calculations becomes efficient and accurate. By following the step-by-step guides and practicing with the practical example, you'll be able to leverage these metrics for meaningful analysis and decision-making. Time-based metrics are powerful tools that enable you to monitor progress and trends over specific periods, enhancing your ability to make data-driven choices.

CHAPTER VIII
Advanced Data Modeling

8.1 Building Relationships between Tables

One of the key strengths of Power BI is its ability to model complex data relationships, enabling you to combine data from multiple tables and sources to gain deeper insights. In this chapter, we will explore the process of building relationships between tables in Power BI, step by step.

Understanding Relationships in Power BI:

Relationships in Power BI allow you to connect tables based on common columns, creating a unified dataset that you can use for analysis. There are three types of relationships: one-to-one, one-to-many, and many-to-many. These relationships form the foundation of your data model.

Step-by-Step Guide to Building Relationships:

Step 1: Import and Load Data:

1. Open Power BI Desktop.

2. Click on "Home" and select "Get Data."

3. Choose the data source(s) you want to import (e.g., Excel, SQL Server, etc.).

4. Follow the prompts to load the data into Power BI.

Step 2: Create a Data Model:

1. In the "Data" view, you will see the tables you imported.

2. Identify the columns that you want to use as keys to establish relationships between tables.

Step 3: Building Relationships:

1. Click on the "Model" view.

2. Drag the column from one table to the matching column in another table.

3. A line will appear between the two tables, indicating the relationship type.

4. A dialog box will appear. Choose the appropriate relationship type (one-to-one, one-to-many, or many-to-many).

5. Optionally, enable "Cross filter direction" if you want the relationship to be bidirectional.

Example: Building a One-to-Many Relationship

Suppose you have two tables: "Sales" and "Products." You want to establish a relationship between them based on the "Product ID" column.

Steps:

1. Import and Load Data:

   - Import the "Sales" and "Products" tables into Power BI.

2. Create a Data Model:

   - Navigate to the "Data" view.

   - Identify the "Product ID" column in both tables.

3. Build the Relationship:

  - Switch to the "Model" view.

  - Drag the "Product ID" column from the "Products" table to the "Product ID" column in the "Sales" table.

  - Select the "Single" arrow option to create a one-to-many relationship.

  - Enable bidirectional cross-filtering if needed.

Important Considerations:

- **Cardinality:** Specify whether the relationship is one-to-one, one-to-many, or many-to-many.

- **Cross Filter Direction:** Decide whether the relationship is unidirectional or bidirectional.

- **Inactive Relationships:** Power BI allows you to have multiple relationships between tables, but only one can be active at a time. You can switch between active and inactive relationships in the "Manage Relationships" window.

Conclusion:

Building relationships between tables is a fundamental skill in Power BI that enhances your data analysis capabilities. By following the step-by-step guide and practicing the provided example, you'll be able to establish effective relationships between tables in your data model. These relationships form the basis for more advanced features like creating meaningful visuals, writing DAX calculations, and generating insights. As you become proficient in building relationships, you'll unlock the full potential of Power BI for data analysis and decision-making.

8.2. Utilizing Calculated Columns and Measures

In Power BI, calculated columns and measures are powerful tools that enable you to perform advanced data modeling and analysis. They allow you to create new data elements based on existing data and perform calculations that provide insights into your data. In this chapter, we will delve into the concepts of calculated columns and measures, provide examples of their usage, and guide you through the process of creating them step by step.

Understanding Calculated Columns:

Calculated columns are user-defined columns that you create in a table. They derive their values from calculations that involve other columns in the same table. Calculated columns are computed at the time of data import and are stored as part of the table. They can be used to create new attributes or perform data transformations.

Creating Calculated Columns:

Step 1: Open Power BI Desktop and Load Data:

1. Launch Power BI Desktop.

2. Click on "Home" and select "Get Data."

3. Choose the data source you want to work with and follow the import process.

Step 2: Create a Calculated Column:

1. Navigate to the "Data" view.

2. Select the table for which you want to create a calculated column.

3. Click on the "Modeling" tab and choose "New Column."

4. Write a DAX formula in the formula bar that defines the calculation for the new column.

Example: Creating a Calculated Column

Let's say you have a "Sales" table with a "Quantity" and "Price" column. You want to create a calculated column for "Total Sales" by multiplying these two columns.

Steps:

1. Open Power BI Desktop and Load Data:

   - Import the "Sales" table into Power BI.

2. Create a Calculated Column:

   - Navigate to the "Data" view.

   - Select the "Sales" table.

   - Click on the "Modeling" tab and choose "New Column."

   - Write the following DAX formula in the formula bar:
     ```

     Total Sales = Sales[Quantity] * Sales[Price]

     ```

3. Use the Calculated Column:

   - Switch to the "Report" view.

   - Add the "Total Sales" column to a table or visualization to see the calculated values.

Understanding Measures:

Measures are calculations that are created at the report level using the Data Analysis Expressions (DAX) language. Measures are used to perform calculations on aggregated data and are particularly useful for creating aggregations, percentages, ratios, and other complex calculations.

Creating Measures:

Step 1: Open Power BI Desktop and Load Data:

1. Launch Power BI Desktop.

2. Click on "Home" and select "Get Data."

3. Choose the data source you want to work with and follow the import process.

Step 2: Create a Measure:

1. Navigate to the "Report" view.

2. Click on the "Modeling" tab and choose "New Measure."

3. Write a DAX formula in the formula bar that defines the calculation for the measure.

Example: Creating a Measure

Continuing with our example, let's create a measure for calculating the "Total Revenue" by summing up the "Total Sales" calculated column.

Steps:

1. Open Power BI Desktop and Load Data:

   - Import the "Sales" table into Power BI.

2. Create a Measure:

   - Navigate to the "Report" view.

   - Click on the "Modeling" tab and choose "New Measure."

   - Write the following DAX formula in the formula bar:

   ```
   ```

   Total Revenue = SUM(Sales[Total Sales])

   ```
   ```

3. Use the Measure:

   - Add the "Total Revenue" measure to a visualization to see the aggregated value.

Key Considerations:

- Calculated Columns vs. Measures: Use calculated columns for calculations that involve individual row values, and measures for calculations that involve aggregated data.

- Performance: Measures are generally more efficient than calculated columns, especially for large datasets.

Conclusion:

Calculated columns and measures are essential components of advanced data modeling in Power BI. By understanding the distinctions between them and following the step-by-step examples provided, you'll be equipped to create powerful calculations that add significant value to your data analysis and reporting. Whether it's performing basic arithmetic or complex statistical operations, the ability to create calculated columns and measures will empower you to extract deeper insights from your data and create more informative visualizations.

8.3. Implementing Hierarchies and Drill-Through

In Power BI, implementing hierarchies and enabling drill-through actions are powerful techniques to enhance your data model and provide users with the ability to navigate and explore data at different levels of detail. Hierarchies allow you to organize related fields into a structured order, while drill-through actions enable users to focus on specific data points and view detailed information. In this chapter, we will explore how to create hierarchies and set up drill-through actions, providing step-by-step instructions and examples for each process.

Creating Hierarchies:

Hierarchies help users analyze data across different levels of granularity, such as year > quarter > month or category > subcategory > product. Here's how you can create hierarchies in Power BI:

Step 1: Open Power BI Desktop and Load Data:

1. Launch Power BI Desktop.

2. Click on "Home" and select "Get Data."

3. Choose the data source you want to work with and follow the import process.

Step 2: Create a Hierarchy:

1. Navigate to the "Model" view.

2. Select the table containing the fields you want to include in the hierarchy.

3. Click on the "Modeling" tab and choose "New Hierarchy."

4. Drag and drop the desired fields into the hierarchy levels, arranging them in the desired order.

Example: Creating a Date Hierarchy

Suppose you have a "Date" table with "Year," "Quarter," and "Month" columns. You want to create a date hierarchy to analyze data at different time levels.

Steps:

1. Open Power BI Desktop and Load Data:

   - Import the "Date" table into Power BI.

2. Create a Date Hierarchy:

   - Navigate to the "Model" view.

   - Select the "Date" table.

   - Click on the "Modeling" tab and choose "New Hierarchy."

   - Drag "Year," "Quarter," and "Month" into the hierarchy levels.

3. Use the Hierarchy:

   - Switch to the "Report" view.

   - Add the date hierarchy to a visualization (e.g., a line chart) to analyze data by year, quarter, and month.

Enabling Drill-Through Actions:

Drill-through actions allow users to view detailed data for a specific data point. For instance, users can click on a sales value to see the individual sales transactions that make up that total. Here's how you can set up drill-through actions in Power BI:

Step 1: Open Power BI Desktop and Load Data:

1. Launch Power BI Desktop.

2. Click on "Home" and select "Get Data."

3. Choose the data source you want to work with and follow the import process.

Step 2: Set Up Drill-Through:

1. Navigate to the "Model" view.

2. Right-click on the field you want to enable drill-through for (e.g., sales amount) and select "New Drillthrough."

3. Choose the related fields you want to include in the drill-through view.

Example: Enabling Drill-Through for Sales Amount

Let's enable drill-through for the "Sales Amount" field in the "Sales" table to see individual sales transactions.

Steps:

1. Open Power BI Desktop and Load Data:

   - Import the "Sales" table into Power BI.

2. Set Up Drill-Through:

- Navigate to the "Model" view.

- Right-click on the "Sales Amount" field.

- Select "New Drillthrough."

- Choose relevant fields like "Product," "Date," and "Customer."

3. Use Drill-Through:

  - Switch to the "Report" view.

  - Add a visualization with the "Sales Amount" field.

  - Right-click on a data point (e.g., a bar in a bar chart) and select "Drill Through."

Key Considerations:

- Hierarchies and User Experience: Hierarchies enhance the user experience by providing organized navigation through data levels.

- Drill-Through and Detail Analysis: Drill-through actions facilitate detailed analysis and allow users to explore data points in-depth.

Conclusion:

By implementing hierarchies and enabling drill-through actions, you empower users to navigate and explore data with ease, gaining insights at different levels of granularity. These advanced data modeling techniques enhance the user experience and enable more interactive and informative reporting. Through step-by-step examples and practical instructions, this chapter equips you with the skills needed to effectively leverage hierarchies and drill-through actions in your Power BI projects, providing a comprehensive understanding of how to organize and interact with complex datasets.

CHAPTER IX
Handling Large Datasets and Performance Optimization

9.1 Techniques for Optimizing Data Load and Refresh

In Power BI, as datasets grow in size and complexity, optimizing data load and refresh processes becomes crucial to ensure smooth performance and responsiveness of your reports and dashboards. This chapter delves into various techniques and strategies for optimizing data load and refresh operations, enabling you to work efficiently with large datasets without sacrificing performance. We'll explore step-by-step procedures and real-world examples to demonstrate the implementation of these optimization techniques.

Understanding Data Load and Refresh Optimization:

Before we delve into specific optimization techniques, it's important to understand the significance of data load and refresh optimization. Power BI enables you to connect to a wide range of data sources, transform the data, and create compelling visuals. However, as datasets expand over time, these operations can slow down, affecting the overall user experience. Optimizing data load and refresh ensures that your reports remain responsive, even when dealing with substantial amounts of data.

Techniques for Optimizing Data Load and Refresh:

1. Data Source Query Optimization:

   - Refine your source queries to fetch only the necessary data, minimizing the amount of data transferred from the source.

- Leverage source query tools and transformations to aggregate and filter data at the source before loading it into Power BI.

2. Data Model Optimization:

- Limit the use of calculated columns, as they can increase data model size and slow down refresh.

- Optimize relationships by avoiding unnecessary bidirectional relationships.

- Use the "Manage Relationships" dialog to control cross-filtering direction and set single-direction filters where applicable.

3. Query Folding:

- Enable query folding whenever possible. Query folding ensures that data transformations are pushed back to the data source, reducing the amount of data transferred to Power BI.

- Use native query folding functions provided by Power Query, such as filtering, sorting, and grouping.

4. Data Partitioning:

- Implement data partitioning for large tables. Partitioning divides the table into smaller, more manageable segments, improving refresh performance.

- Utilize partitioning strategies based on date ranges or meaningful divisions in your data.

5. Incremental Load:

- Implement incremental data loading to refresh only new or changed data, reducing refresh times for large datasets.

- Combine Power Query's date filtering capabilities with incremental refresh settings in Power BI Service.

6. Data Compression:

- Utilize data compression options available in Power BI to reduce data model size without sacrificing data quality.

- Experiment with different compression settings to find the right balance between performance and storage.

Example: Optimizing Data Load for a Large Sales Dataset

Suppose you are working with a sales dataset containing millions of records. Here's how you can optimize data load and refresh for this dataset:

Steps:

1. Data Source Query Optimization:

- In your data source query, apply filters to fetch only relevant data, such as a specific date range or product category.

2. Data Model Optimization:

- Avoid unnecessary calculated columns that might slow down the data model.

- Optimize relationships by removing bidirectional relationships that are not required.

3. Query Folding:

- Use Power Query to apply filtering and grouping operations in your source query, promoting query folding.

4. Data Partitioning:

- Partition the sales table based on months to create smaller segments.

- Set up partitioning in the Power BI data source settings.

5. Incremental Load:

  - Implement incremental refresh to load only new sales transactions.

  - Configure the incremental refresh settings in Power BI Service.

6. Data Compression:

  - Experiment with different compression settings for the data model to reduce its size.

Key Considerations:

- **Balancing Performance and Functionality:** While optimizing data load and refresh is crucial, it's essential to strike a balance between performance and the need for complex transformations and calculations.

- **Regular Maintenance:** Periodically review and optimize your data load and refresh processes as your dataset evolves.

Conclusion:

Optimizing data load and refresh operations is paramount to ensure the optimal performance of your Power BI reports and dashboards. By implementing the techniques outlined in this chapter, you'll be equipped to handle large datasets efficiently and maintain the responsiveness of your analytics solutions. Through practical examples and step-by-step instructions, this chapter empowers you to navigate the complexities of data optimization, enabling you to deliver impactful visualizations and insights to your users while maintaining an excellent user experience.

9.2. Implementing Incremental Data Refresh Strategies

When dealing with large datasets in Power BI, implementing incremental data refresh strategies can significantly enhance performance and streamline the data loading process. This chapter focuses on the concept of incremental refresh, its benefits, and how to implement various incremental data refresh strategies using Power BI. We will walk through step-by-step procedures, provide practical examples, and guide you on choosing the right strategy based on your dataset and requirements.

Understanding Incremental Data Refresh:

Incremental data refresh is a technique that enables you to refresh only the new or modified data in your dataset, rather than reloading the entire dataset. This is particularly useful for datasets that grow over time, as it helps reduce refresh times and optimizes the overall data loading process.

Benefits of Incremental Data Refresh:

- **Faster Refresh:** By refreshing only a subset of data, the refresh process becomes faster and more efficient.

- **Reduced Resource Consumption:** Incremental refresh minimizes the strain on your data source and Power BI Service resources.

- **Consistency:** Reports remain up-to-date while reducing the risk of errors introduced during refresh.

Implementing Incremental Data Refresh Strategies:

1. Identifying Key Fields: Determine the fields that can be used to identify new or modified records. Typically, a timestamp or an incremental key is used for this purpose.

2. Creating a Marker Table: Build a separate table to store the latest refresh timestamp or the maximum incremental key value. This table will serve as a reference point for identifying new data.

3. Configuring Incremental Refresh:

  - In Power BI Desktop, navigate to "File" > "Options and settings" > "Options" > "Data Load."

  - Enable "Incremental Refresh" and specify the marker table and key fields.

  - Set up partitioning by defining ranges based on the key field values.

4. Publishing to Power BI Service:

  - Publish your report to Power BI Service.

  - Configure incremental refresh settings in the dataset settings.

  - Specify the refresh frequency and the number of days to keep data.

5. Testing and Monitoring:

  - Test the incremental refresh by manually triggering a refresh and verifying the results.

  - Monitor refresh performance, resource consumption, and data accuracy over time.

Example: Implementing Incremental Refresh for Sales Data

Suppose you have a sales dataset with daily transactions. Here's how you can implement incremental refresh:

Steps:

1. Identifying Key Fields: In your sales data, identify a "TransactionDate" field as the key field to track new data.

2. Creating a Marker Table: Create a separate table named "RefreshMetadata" with a single column "LastRefreshDate."

3. Configuring Incremental Refresh:

- In Power BI Desktop, enable incremental refresh and select the "RefreshMetadata" table as the marker table.

- Choose "TransactionDate" as the key column for partitioning.

4. Publishing to Power BI Service:

- Publish the report to Power BI Service.

- Configure incremental refresh settings by specifying the refresh frequency and retention policy.

5. Testing and Monitoring:

- Manually trigger a refresh in Power BI Service and observe the refresh duration.

- Regularly monitor refresh performance and validate data accuracy.

Key Considerations:

- Data Source Limitations: Incremental refresh may not be suitable for all data sources. Ensure that your data source supports the necessary operations for incremental refresh.

- Data Model Complexity: Incremental refresh is most effective for datasets that are updated with new records over time. For datasets with frequent structural changes, consider other optimization strategies.

Conclusion:

Implementing incremental data refresh strategies is a valuable approach to handling large datasets and optimizing data loading processes in Power BI. By following the outlined steps and considering the example provided, you can seamlessly incorporate incremental refresh into your data transformation workflow. This chapter empowers you with the knowledge and practical guidance needed to enhance performance, reduce refresh times, and ensure the accuracy of your reports and dashboards, even as your dataset continues to grow.

9.3. Utilizing Data Compression and Aggregation

Handling large datasets efficiently is crucial for maintaining optimal performance in Power BI. This chapter delves into the techniques of data compression and aggregation, which are powerful strategies for reducing memory consumption, improving query performance, and ensuring smooth interactions with your reports and dashboards. We will explore how to implement these techniques, provide real-world examples, and guide you through step-by-step instructions to harness the benefits of data compression and aggregation.

Understanding Data Compression:

Data compression is the process of reducing the amount of storage space required for your dataset while maintaining its integrity. In Power BI, compression techniques can significantly improve performance by minimizing memory usage and speeding up query execution.

Benefits of Data Compression:

- Faster Query Performance: Compressed data requires less time to load and query, resulting in faster report rendering.

- Lower Resource Consumption: Compressed datasets consume less memory and reduce strain on your system resources.

- Enhanced User Experience: Users can interact with reports and dashboards more smoothly due to reduced latency.

Implementing Data Compression:

1. Choosing the Right Compression Strategy:

  - Identify columns with high cardinality and repetitive values, as they are prime candidates for compression.

  - Evaluate the nature of your data (numeric, textual, categorical) to determine the most suitable compression technique.

2. Applying Data Types and Encodings:

  - Utilize appropriate data types that require less storage space (e.g., using INT instead of BIGINT for smaller ranges).

  - Leverage encoding methods like dictionary encoding for categorical columns and delta encoding for sorted data.

3. Utilizing Compression Algorithms:

  - Power BI employs columnar compression techniques (such as Run Length and Dictionary encoding) to compress data efficiently.

  - Be aware that compression may impact CPU usage during data refresh and query execution.

Example: Compressing a Sales Dataset

Suppose you have a sales dataset with various columns, including "ProductID," "Category," "SalesAmount," and "OrderDate." Here's how you can apply data compression:

Steps:

1. Choosing the Right Compression Strategy:

  - Identify columns with repetitive or categorical data, such as "Category."

  - Prioritize columns that have a high number of duplicate values.

2. Applying Data Types and Encodings:

  - Change the data type of "ProductID" and "SalesAmount" to INT if they fit within the INT range.

  - Convert the "Category" column to a categorical data type.

3. Utilizing Compression Algorithms:

  - Power BI automatically applies appropriate compression techniques, so no manual configuration is needed.

Understanding Data Aggregation:

Data aggregation involves summarizing and consolidating data to reduce the overall volume of information while retaining its essential insights. Aggregated data is particularly useful for visualizations that require high-level trends and patterns.

Benefits of Data Aggregation:

- Improved Query Performance: Aggregated data requires fewer calculations, resulting in faster query execution.

- Simplified Visualizations: Aggregated data can simplify complex visualizations and reduce visual clutter.

- Reduced Memory Usage: Smaller data size due to aggregation contributes to reduced memory consumption.

Implementing Data Aggregation:

1. Identifying Aggregation Levels:

  - Determine the granularity at which data should be aggregated (e.g., daily, monthly, quarterly).

  - Identify key metrics that need to be aggregated, such as total sales or average revenue.

2. Creating Aggregation Tables:

  - Create new tables or views that store aggregated data based on the identified levels and metrics.

  - Use DAX functions like SUMMARIZE to generate aggregated tables.

3. Utilizing Aggregated Data in Visualizations:

  - Use the aggregated tables in your reports to create high-level visualizations.

  - Link aggregated tables to other tables using relationships for more comprehensive insights.

Example: Creating Monthly Sales Aggregates

Suppose you have a detailed sales dataset with daily transactions. Here's how you can implement data aggregation:

Steps:

1. Identifying Aggregation Levels:

  - Choose "Monthly" as the aggregation level for the "OrderDate" field.

2. Creating Aggregation Tables:

  - Create a new table named "MonthlySales" with columns "Year," "Month," and aggregated metrics like "TotalSales."

  - Use the SUMMARIZE function to aggregate data by year and month.

3. Utilizing Aggregated Data in Visualizations:

  - Create visualizations using the "MonthlySales" table to showcase monthly trends.

  - Connect the "MonthlySales" table to the main sales table using the "Year" and "Month" columns.

Key Considerations:

- Balance Between Detail and Aggregation: While aggregation enhances performance, ensure that you maintain the right balance between aggregated and detailed data for comprehensive analysis.

- Dynamic Aggregation: Utilize Power BI's capabilities to allow users to dynamically switch between detailed and aggregated views.

CHAPTER X
Power BI Gateway and On-Premises Data

10.1 Connecting to On-Premises Data Sources

In many organizations, data resides within on-premises sources such as databases, files, and applications. Power BI allows you to seamlessly connect and refresh data from these sources using the Power BI Gateway. This chapter explores the process of connecting to on-premises data sources, configuring the Power BI Gateway, and establishing secure and efficient data flows between your local environment and Power BI service.

Understanding On-Premises Data Connectivity:

On-premises data connectivity refers to the ability to establish a secure and reliable connection between Power BI and data sources that are not hosted in the cloud. This is essential for maintaining up-to-date data in your Power BI reports and dashboards, especially when dealing with sensitive or large datasets that need to stay within your organization's network.

Benefits of On-Premises Data Connectivity:

- **Real-time Data Updates:** On-premises data connectivity ensures that your Power BI reports reflect the latest information from your local databases and systems.

- **Data Security:** Sensitive data can be kept within your organization's firewall, ensuring compliance with security policies.

- **Flexible Reporting:** You can create rich visualizations and reports using on-premises data, combining it with cloud-based data for comprehensive insights.

Connecting to On-Premises Data Sources:

1. Install and Configure Power BI Gateway:

  - Download and install the Power BI Gateway, available from the Power BI service.

  - Configure the gateway by signing in with your Power BI account and selecting the appropriate on-premises data sources to connect.

2. Connecting to Data Sources:

  - Open Power BI Desktop and click on "Get Data."

  - Choose the relevant data source type, such as SQL Server, Oracle, SharePoint, or file sources like Excel or CSV.

3. Configuring Connection Settings:

  - Enter the server name, database name, and credentials for database sources.

  - Specify the file path and format for file-based sources.

4. Customizing Data Query:

  - Utilize Power Query Editor to transform and shape data as needed before importing into Power BI.

Example: Connecting to an On-Premises SQL Server Database

Let's walk through the process of connecting to an on-premises SQL Server database using Power BI Gateway:

Steps:

1. Install and Configure Power BI Gateway:

- Download and install the Power BI Gateway on a machine that has access to the SQL Server database.

2. Connecting to Data Source:

- Open Power BI Desktop and click on "Get Data."

- Select "SQL Server Database" from the list of data sources.

3. Configuring Connection Settings:

- Enter the server name and database name.

- Choose the appropriate authentication method (Windows or database credentials) and provide the necessary credentials.

4. Importing Data:

- Select the tables or views you want to import.

- Use the "Transform Data" option to apply any necessary data transformations using Power Query Editor.

5. Publish to Power BI Service:

- Save your Power BI Desktop file and publish it to the Power BI service.

- Configure the dataset to use the on-premises gateway for data refresh.

Ensuring Data Security:

- Gateway Configuration: Ensure the Power BI Gateway is configured correctly and associated with your Power BI account.

- Data Source Permissions: Set appropriate permissions on the on-premises data sources for the gateway to access.

Conclusion:

Connecting to on-premises data sources using Power BI Gateway enables you to leverage the benefits of Power BI while keeping your sensitive data within your organization's network. By following the steps outlined in this chapter and leveraging the Power BI Gateway, you can establish a seamless data flow between your on-premises data sources and the Power BI service, ensuring that your reports and dashboards are always up to date and accurate.

10.2. Configuring and Managing Power BI Gateway

The Power BI Gateway serves as a bridge between your on-premises data sources and the Power BI service in the cloud. Configuring and managing the gateway effectively is crucial to ensuring smooth and secure data connectivity. This chapter delves into the process of setting up, configuring, and managing the Power BI Gateway for seamless on-premises data integration.

Installing and Setting Up Power BI Gateway:

1. Download and Install:

  - Visit the Power BI service and download the Power BI Gateway appropriate for your environment (personal or enterprise).

  - Run the installation package and follow the prompts to install the gateway software.

2. Sign In to Power BI:

- Launch the Power BI Gateway application and sign in with your Power BI account.

- You'll be prompted to create a new gateway or use an existing one.

Configuring Data Sources:

1. Add Data Sources:

- In the Power BI Gateway application, navigate to the "Manage Gateways" section.

- Click on "Add Data Source" and select the type of data source (e.g., SQL Server, Oracle, File Share).

2. Connection Details:

- Provide the necessary connection details, such as server name, database name, authentication credentials, and folder paths.

- Test the connection to ensure it's successful.

Customizing Gateway Settings:

1. Data Source Credentials:

- Define how credentials are stored and used for data sources (individual user or single set of credentials).

2. Gateway Cluster Mode:

- Choose between "Standard Mode" (single gateway) and "Personal Mode" (user-specific gateways).

3. High Availability Configuration:

KIET HUYNH

- Configure failover and redundancy options to ensure continuous data connectivity.

Managing and Monitoring Gateway:

1. Gateway Status:

   - Monitor the status of your gateway(s) from the Power BI service.

   - Ensure that the gateway is online and connected to the Power BI service.

2. Data Source Permissions:

   - Manage permissions for data sources by defining who can access and refresh data using the gateway.

3. Troubleshooting:

   - Utilize diagnostic tools to troubleshoot connectivity issues between the gateway and data sources.

Example: Configuring a Power BI Gateway for SQL Server

Let's go through the steps to set up and configure a Power BI Gateway for connecting to an on-premises SQL Server database:

Steps:

1. Download and Install Gateway:

   - Download the Power BI Gateway installer from the Power BI service.

   - Run the installer and follow the setup instructions.

2. Sign In and Create Gateway:

- Open the Power BI Gateway application and sign in with your Power BI account.

- Choose to create a new gateway and provide a name.

3. Add Data Source:

- Navigate to "Manage Gateways" and click on "Add Data Source."

- Select "SQL Server" and provide connection details (server name, database name, authentication).

4. Customize Settings:

- Configure data source credentials and gateway mode (standard or personal).

- Set up high availability if needed.

5. Gateway Monitoring:

- Monitor the gateway status from the Power BI service.

- Verify that the gateway is connected and data sources are accessible.

Conclusion:

Configuring and managing the Power BI Gateway is a critical step in establishing secure and efficient data connectivity between on-premises sources and the Power BI service. By following the steps outlined in this chapter and tailoring the configuration to your organization's needs, you can ensure that your on-premises data is seamlessly integrated with Power BI, enabling you to create insightful reports and dashboards that provide valuable insights.

10.3. Maintaining Data Security and Privacy

Ensuring the security and privacy of your data is of paramount importance when connecting Power BI to on-premises data sources through the Power BI Gateway. This chapter explores best practices for maintaining data security and privacy while utilizing the gateway, along with practical steps to implement these measures effectively.

Securing Data Transfer:

1. Encryption:

- Enable encryption for data transfer between the Power BI Gateway and the on-premises data sources.

- Configure SSL certificates to ensure secure communication.

2. Data Privacy Levels:

- Define data privacy levels to restrict data access based on user roles and data source sensitivity.

- Utilize the "Combine" option to control data blending from different sources.

Implementing Authentication and Authorization:

1. Gateway Credentials:

- Store gateway credentials securely to prevent unauthorized access.

- Limit access to individuals who require data refresh capabilities.

2. Data Source Credentials:

- Implement strong authentication methods (e.g., Windows authentication, OAuth) for data source connections.

- Avoid using generic or shared credentials.

3. User Mapping:

- Map users in the Power BI service to appropriate roles in the on-premises data sources.

- Ensure that users only access the data they are authorized to see.

Auditing and Monitoring:

1. Gateway Logs:

- Regularly review gateway logs to monitor user activities and diagnose potential security issues.

- Set up alerts for suspicious activities.

2. Usage Metrics:

- Monitor data refresh and query usage patterns to identify anomalies or unusual behavior.

Example: Implementing Data Privacy and Security for an Oracle Database

Let's consider an example of maintaining data security and privacy while connecting to an on-premises Oracle database:

Steps:

1. Enable Encryption:

- Configure SSL encryption for communication between the Power BI Gateway and Oracle database.

2. Define Data Privacy Levels:

- Classify data sources based on sensitivity (e.g., public, confidential, highly confidential).

- Set data privacy levels to restrict data blending between different sensitivity levels.

3. Strong Authentication:

- Implement Windows authentication for Oracle database access.

- Utilize Oracle Wallet for secure password storage.

4. User Mapping and Authorization:

- Map Power BI users to specific roles in the Oracle database.

- Define object-level permissions to limit data access.

5. Gateway Logs and Alerts:

- Regularly review gateway logs for data refresh and query activities.

- Configure alerts for any unauthorized or abnormal activities.

Conclusion:

Maintaining data security and privacy is a critical aspect of using the Power BI Gateway to connect to on-premises data sources. By implementing encryption, strong authentication, data privacy levels, and effective monitoring, you can ensure that your organization's data remains secure and compliant while benefiting from the insights provided by Power BI reports and dashboards. It is essential to tailor these security measures to your organization's specific requirements and continually update them to stay ahead of potential security risks.

CHAPTER XI
Data Transformation Best Practices

11.1 Designing Efficient and Maintainable Queries

Efficient and maintainable data transformation queries are crucial for ensuring optimal performance and long-term manageability of your Power BI projects. This chapter delves into key principles and strategies for designing queries that are both efficient in terms of processing time and easy to maintain over time.

1. Start with a Clear Objective:

Begin your query design by clearly defining the goal of the transformation. Determine the specific data you need and the desired outcome of the transformation. This helps you avoid unnecessary steps and reduces processing overhead.

2. Minimize Data Movement:

Efficient queries minimize data movement between steps. Whenever possible, perform transformations within the same step using built-in functions and operations. Reducing data movement enhances performance by avoiding unnecessary data transfers.

3. Filter Early:

Apply filters and data reduction operations as early as possible in the query. This reduces the amount of data that needs to be processed in subsequent steps. For example, if you are working with a large dataset, apply filtering operations in the initial steps to narrow down the scope.

4. Avoid Unnecessary Columns:

Select only the columns you need for your analysis. Removing unnecessary columns early in the transformation process reduces memory consumption and processing time. This is especially important when dealing with large datasets.

5. Optimize Data Types:

Use appropriate data types for columns to reduce memory usage and improve query performance. For example, use integer data types for whole numbers and date/time data types for date-related values.

6. Utilize Query Folding:

Leverage query folding whenever possible. Query folding allows Power Query to push transformation operations back to the data source, optimizing performance. Monitor query folding by checking the "Applied Steps" window for each query.

7. Merge Queries Efficiently:

When merging queries, use the least resource-intensive join operations (e.g., inner join) and avoid unnecessary duplication of data. Utilize indexing in source data to speed up merge operations.

8. Split Complex Transformations:

For complex transformations, consider breaking them into smaller, manageable steps. This improves query readability and makes it easier to troubleshoot and maintain the query over time.

9. Document and Comment:

Document your queries and add comments to explain each step's purpose and logic. This helps other team members understand the query and simplifies maintenance.

10. Test and Validate:

Regularly test and validate your queries with different data scenarios to ensure accuracy and optimal performance. Use the Query Diagnostics feature to identify performance bottlenecks.

Example: Designing an Efficient Query for Sales Data

Let's say you are working with a large sales dataset and need to calculate the total revenue for each product category. Here's how you can design an efficient query:

Steps:

1. Load the sales data into Power Query.

2. Filter the data to include only the relevant columns (e.g., ProductID, Category, SalesAmount, Date).

3. Group the data by Category using the Group By operation, summing the SalesAmount.

4. Rename columns and create a new column for total revenue.

5. Load the transformed data into your Power BI model.

Conclusion:

Designing efficient and maintainable queries is crucial for optimizing the performance and manageability of your Power BI projects. By following best practices such as filtering early, optimizing data types, leveraging query folding, and breaking down complex transformations, you can ensure that your queries deliver accurate insights while minimizing processing time and resource consumption. Regular testing, documentation, and validation are key to maintaining query efficiency over time.

11.2. Documenting and Sharing Data Transformation Steps

Documenting and sharing data transformation steps is essential for maintaining transparency, collaboration, and knowledge sharing within your Power BI projects. Proper documentation helps ensure that team members can understand, replicate, and troubleshoot your data transformations effectively. This chapter explores the importance of documenting your data transformation processes and provides guidelines for sharing these steps with your team.

1. Why Document Data Transformation Steps:

Clear documentation provides several benefits:

- **Transparency:** Documentation allows team members to understand how data transformations are performed, promoting transparency and reducing ambiguity.

- **Collaboration:** Proper documentation enables multiple team members to work on the same project efficiently by sharing insights into the data transformation logic.

- **Troubleshooting:** In case of issues or errors, well-documented steps facilitate the identification and resolution of problems.

2. Documenting Data Transformation Steps:

Follow these steps to effectively document your data transformation process:

a. Step Descriptions: Provide clear and concise descriptions for each transformation step. Explain the purpose of the step, the logic applied, and any assumptions made.

b. Naming Conventions: Use consistent and meaningful names for each step to make it easy for others to understand the purpose of the transformation.

c. Comments: Add comments within the Power Query Editor to explain specific parts of the transformation logic. Comments provide context and insights for others who review the query.

d. Inline Documentation: If necessary, create a separate sheet or document that explains the overall data transformation process, including an overview of the steps involved.

3. Sharing Data Transformation Steps:

Sharing your data transformation steps with your team involves communication and collaboration. Consider the following methods:

a. Shared Repository: Use version control tools like Git to maintain a shared repository where team members can access, review, and contribute to the data transformation queries.

b. Team Collaboration Tools: Utilize collaboration platforms like Microsoft Teams or Slack to share the data transformation process with your team. You can create dedicated channels for discussing queries and transformations.

c. Documentation Platforms: Use documentation platforms like Confluence or SharePoint to create comprehensive documentation for your data transformation processes.

4. Example: Documenting and Sharing Steps for Cleaning Customer Data:

Let's consider an example where you're cleaning customer data for a sales analysis project:

Steps:

1. Load Data: Load customer data from a CSV file.

2. Remove Duplicates: Remove duplicate records based on customer ID.

3. Handle Null Values: Replace null values in the "Age" column with the average age.

4. Standardize Names: Convert customer names to title case for consistency.

5. Calculate Age Groups: Create age groups (e.g., "18-30," "31-45," etc.) based on age.

6. Filter Irrelevant Columns: Remove columns not needed for analysis.

7. Rename Columns: Provide descriptive names for columns.

8. Load Cleaned Data: Load the cleaned data into the Power BI model.

Sharing: Upload the Power Query script and a document explaining each step to your team's documentation platform.

Conclusion:

Documenting and sharing data transformation steps is a crucial aspect of maintaining effective collaboration and transparency within your Power BI projects. By providing clear step descriptions, using consistent naming conventions, adding comments, and leveraging collaboration tools, you ensure that team members can understand, replicate, and contribute to data transformations effectively. Sharing your documented steps through shared repositories, collaboration platforms, or documentation platforms enhances teamwork and knowledge sharing, ultimately leading to better insights and decision-making.

11.3. Troubleshooting and Error Handling

Efficient troubleshooting and error handling are fundamental skills in any data transformation process. This chapter delves into the strategies and best practices for identifying and addressing errors that may occur during data transformation in Power BI. We'll explore common types of errors, techniques for troubleshooting, and effective error handling methods to ensure the accuracy and reliability of your transformed data.

1. Identifying Common Errors:

Before diving into troubleshooting and error handling, let's familiarize ourselves with some common errors that may arise during data transformation:

a. Data Format Errors: Incompatible data formats between columns or sources can lead to errors.

b. Null Value Handling: Mishandling of null values can cause issues in calculations and aggregations.

c. Incorrect Join Conditions: Errors may occur due to incorrect join conditions between tables.

d. Formula Syntax Errors: Improperly written formulas or DAX expressions can lead to errors.

2. Techniques for Troubleshooting:

When errors occur during data transformation, consider the following techniques for effective troubleshooting:

a. Query Diagnostics: Power Query provides tools to diagnose errors. Use the "View" tab to access the "Query Diagnostics" option, which shows a detailed breakdown of applied steps and errors.

b. Query Dependencies: The "Query Dependencies" view helps identify dependencies between queries, making it easier to trace back errors to their sources.

c. Error Messages: Carefully read error messages provided by Power Query. They often contain valuable information about the nature of the error.

d. Step-by-Step Review: Review each step in your transformation process to pinpoint where an error might have occurred.

3. Error Handling Best Practices:

Implementing robust error handling techniques ensures that your data transformation processes can recover gracefully from errors. Here's how:

a. Conditional Logic: Use conditional logic to handle specific error scenarios. For example, you can replace null values with defaults or skip problematic rows.

b. Try-Catch Statements: In Power Query, you can use try-catch expressions to handle errors within custom functions or expressions.

c. Error Output Handling: Configure error output options for specific steps. You can choose to replace errors with specific values or remove them altogether.

d. Custom Error Messages: Create custom error messages to provide more meaningful explanations to users encountering errors.

4. Example: Handling Null Values in Age Column:

Let's consider an example where you're dealing with null values in an "Age" column:

Step 1: Load the data into Power Query.

Step 2: Use the "Replace Values" transformation to replace null values in the "Age" column with a default value (e.g., 30).

Step 3: Implement a conditional logic step to flag rows where the age is still null after replacement.

5. Sharing Troubleshooting Guidelines:

To foster collaboration and knowledge sharing within your team, consider creating a troubleshooting guide that outlines the process for identifying and addressing common errors. This guide can include step-by-step instructions for diagnosing issues, suggested solutions, and examples.

Conclusion:

Effective troubleshooting and error handling are essential components of a successful data transformation process in Power BI. By understanding common errors, using diagnostic tools, and implementing error handling best practices, you can ensure the accuracy and reliability of your transformed data. Through careful analysis and problem-solving, you'll be well-equipped to navigate and resolve any issues that arise, ultimately leading to more accurate and insightful reports and visualizations.

CHAPTER XII
Case Studies and Real-World Examples

12.1 Retail Sales Analysis: From Raw Data to Insights

In this chapter, we will dive into a comprehensive case study that demonstrates how to transform raw retail sales data into actionable insights using Power BI. This real-world example will guide you through the entire data transformation process, from importing and cleaning the data to creating advanced visualizations for meaningful analysis.

1. Understanding the Scenario:

Imagine you are a business analyst tasked with analyzing retail sales data to gain insights into product performance, customer behavior, and sales trends. The data comes in the form of a CSV file containing information about sales transactions, products, customers, and dates.

2. Importing and Loading Data:

Begin by importing the raw retail sales data into Power BI:

Step 1: Open Power BI Desktop.

Step 2: Click on "Home" > "Get Data" > "CSV" and select the CSV file.

Step 3: Choose the appropriate delimiter and format settings.

Step 4: Preview the data and click "Load" to import it.

3. Data Cleaning and Preparation:

Before you can derive insights from the data, you need to clean and prepare it:

Step 1: Explore the data to identify missing values, outliers, and inconsistencies.

Step 2: Remove duplicate rows using the "Remove Duplicates" feature.

Step 3: Handle missing values by replacing them with appropriate defaults or applying interpolation techniques.

Step 4: Convert data types if necessary (e.g., converting date columns to proper date format).

4. Creating Relationships:

Establish relationships between tables to enable meaningful analysis:

Step 1: Click on "Model" > "Diagram View."

Step 2: Drag and drop fields from different tables to create relationships.

Step 3: Set relationship properties such as cardinality and cross-filtering direction.

5. Data Transformation and Aggregation:

Use Power Query to perform data transformation and aggregation for analysis:

Step 1: Click on "Transform Data" to open the Power Query Editor.

Step 2: Apply data transformation steps like filtering, sorting, and grouping.

Step 3: Create calculated columns and measures using DAX expressions.

Step 4: Aggregate data to create key metrics such as total sales, average order value, and customer segmentation.

6. Building Visualizations:

Now it's time to create insightful visualizations based on the transformed data:

Step 1: Return to the main Power BI window.

Step 2: Drag and drop visual elements like charts, tables, and slicers onto the canvas.

Step 3: Customize visual properties, colors, and labels for clarity.

Step 4: Use the "Format" and "Analytics" tabs to enhance visualizations with additional features and insights.

7. Deriving Insights:

With your visualizations in place, start extracting valuable insights:

Step 1: Analyze sales trends over time using line charts or area charts.

Step 2: Explore product performance by category, subcategory, or brand using bar charts or scatter plots.

Step 3: Use slicers to enable interactive filtering and drill-down analysis.

Step 4: Create a dashboard with multiple visualizations to provide a holistic view of the retail sales data.

8. Sharing and Collaboration:

Finally, share your insights with stakeholders for collaborative decision-making:

Step 1: Publish the report to the Power BI service.

Step 2: Share the report with specific users or groups.

Step 3: Enable data-driven alerts to notify stakeholders of significant changes.

Step 4: Use the Power BI service's collaboration features for discussions and annotations.

Conclusion:

This case study showcases how to transform raw retail sales data into actionable insights using Power BI. By following the step-by-step process of importing, cleaning, transforming, visualizing, and sharing data, you can apply similar techniques to various real-world scenarios. The skills you've gained throughout this book will empower you to confidently tackle data transformation challenges and derive valuable insights from your data using the power of Power BI.

12.2. Financial Data Transformation and Reporting

In this case study, we will delve into the process of transforming complex financial data and creating insightful reports using Power BI. Financial data is often intricate and requires meticulous handling to derive meaningful insights. Through this real-world example, you will learn how to import, clean, transform, and visualize financial data to generate accurate and actionable reports.

1. Understanding the Scenario:

Imagine you are a financial analyst tasked with analyzing and reporting on the financial performance of a company. The data is sourced from various financial systems, including accounting software, spreadsheets, and databases. Your goal is to transform this data into a format that facilitates effective financial analysis and reporting.

2. Importing and Loading Financial Data:

Begin by importing the diverse financial data into Power BI:

Step 1: Open Power BI Desktop.

Step 2: Click on "Home" > "Get Data" to select the appropriate data sources, such as Excel, SQL Server, or online services.

Step 3: Connect to the financial data sources by providing necessary credentials or connection details.

Step 4: Load the data into Power BI.

3. Cleaning and Transforming Financial Data:

Effective financial analysis hinges on clean and well-structured data:

Step 1: Identify and address missing values, outliers, and inconsistencies in the financial data.

Step 2: Standardize and cleanse account names, transaction descriptions, and other relevant fields.

Step 3: Combine data from different sources by merging or appending queries.

Step 4: Apply data transformation techniques to pivot, unpivot, or aggregate data for analysis.

4. Financial Calculations and Metrics:

Transform raw financial data into actionable metrics and KPIs:

Step 1: Use DAX (Data Analysis Expressions) to create financial calculations like revenue, expenses, net income, and profit margins.

Step 2: Generate financial ratios such as current ratio, debt-to-equity ratio, and return on investment (ROI).

Step 3: Implement time-based calculations like year-to-date (YTD) and quarter-to-date (QTD) comparisons.

Step 4: Utilize DAX functions for currency conversion and inflation adjustment.

5. Building Financial Reports:

Translate transformed financial data into visually informative reports:

Step 1: Design financial reports by selecting appropriate visualizations such as tables, line charts, bar charts, and KPI cards.

Step 2: Create financial dashboards with multiple pages to provide a comprehensive view of the company's financial performance.

Step 3: Leverage slicers and filters to enable users to interactively explore financial data.

Step 4: Implement drill-through actions to allow users to dive deeper into specific financial metrics.

6. Budgeting and Forecasting:

Enhance your financial analysis by incorporating budgeting and forecasting:

Step 1: Import budget data from spreadsheets or dedicated budgeting software.

Step 2: Compare actual financial performance to budgeted figures using variance analysis.

Step 3: Implement forecasting techniques to project future financial trends based on historical data.

Step 4: Visualize budgeted and forecasted values alongside actual performance for comprehensive analysis.

7. Sharing and Collaboration:

Share your financial reports and insights with relevant stakeholders:

Step 1: Publish the financial report to the Power BI service.

Step 2: Create and configure dashboards for different user groups, such as executives, managers, and analysts.

Step 3: Schedule automatic data refresh to ensure reports reflect the most up-to-date financial information.

Step 4: Collaborate with stakeholders by enabling comments, annotations, and discussions within the Power BI service.

Conclusion:

This case study demonstrates the end-to-end process of transforming complex financial data into insightful reports using Power BI. By mastering the techniques of importing, cleaning, transforming, calculating, and visualizing financial data, you can effectively analyze financial performance, make informed decisions, and drive business growth. The skills you've acquired throughout this book will empower you to handle intricate financial data with confidence and produce valuable financial reports using the power of Power BI.

12.3. Social Media Analytics with Power BI

In this case study, we'll delve into the exciting world of social media analytics and explore how Power BI can be used to transform raw social media data into valuable insights. Social media platforms generate massive amounts of data daily, containing valuable information about customer sentiment, engagement, and trends. By harnessing the capabilities of Power BI, you can unlock these insights and make data-driven decisions for your business.

1. Defining the Objective:

Let's imagine you work for a marketing agency that manages social media campaigns for various clients. Your goal is to analyze and visualize social media data to measure campaign performance, understand audience behavior, and optimize strategies.

2. Collecting and Preparing Social Media Data:

Start by collecting data from various social media platforms:

Step 1: Access the APIs of social media platforms like Facebook, Twitter, and Instagram to retrieve data such as posts, comments, likes, shares, and followers.

Step 2: Import the collected data into Power BI by using methods like API connectors or exporting data to CSV files.

Step 3: Cleanse and prepare the data by addressing missing values, removing duplicates, and standardizing formats.

3. Sentiment Analysis and Engagement Metrics:

Understand customer sentiment and measure engagement with your social media content:

Step 1: Utilize Natural Language Processing (NLP) techniques to perform sentiment analysis on text data such as comments and posts.

Step 2: Calculate engagement metrics like likes per post, comments per post, and shares per post.

Step 3: Visualize sentiment trends and engagement metrics over time using line charts or area charts.

4. Audience Segmentation and Demographics:

Segment your audience and uncover demographic insights:

Step 1: Analyze follower demographics such as age, gender, location, and interests.

Step 2: Use Power Query to clean and transform demographic data for accurate analysis.

Step 3: Create demographic segments and visualize them using pie charts, bar charts, or maps.

5. Hashtag and Content Analysis:

Understand the impact of hashtags and content on engagement:

Step 1: Extract hashtags from posts and perform hashtag analysis to identify trending topics.

Step 2: Analyze the performance of different types of content, such as images, videos, and articles.

Step 3: Visualize hashtag trends and content performance using bar charts and scatter plots.

6. Influencer and Competitor Analysis:

Identify key influencers and benchmark against competitors:

Step 1: Analyze user engagement and follower counts to identify top influencers.

Step 2: Benchmark your performance against competitors by comparing engagement metrics.

Step 3: Create visuals that showcase influencer and competitor insights side by side.

7. Dashboard Creation and Sharing:

Compile your social media insights into an interactive dashboard:

Step 1: Design a comprehensive dashboard with visuals that represent different aspects of social media performance.

Step 2: Use slicers and filters to enable users to explore specific time periods, platforms, or content types.

Step 3: Share the dashboard with clients or team members using the Power BI service.

Conclusion:

This case study showcases the application of Power BI in social media analytics, highlighting the process of collecting, analyzing, and visualizing social media data to make informed marketing decisions. By following the steps outlined in this example, you can effectively measure the success of your social media campaigns, gain insights into audience behavior, and optimize your strategies for maximum impact. Power BI's capabilities enable you to turn raw social media data into actionable insights that drive business growth and enhance your marketing efforts.

CHAPTER XIII
Future Trends in Data Transformation

13.1 Exploring the Evolving Landscape of Data Transformation

As the field of data transformation continues to evolve, staying ahead of emerging trends is crucial for data professionals and organizations seeking to extract meaningful insights from their data. This chapter explores some of the key future trends in data transformation, providing insights into where the industry is headed and how you can prepare to harness these advancements.

1. Automated Data Transformation:

The future of data transformation lies in automation. With the rise of artificial intelligence (AI) and machine learning (ML), data transformation processes are becoming more intelligent and automated. Tools and platforms are being developed to analyze data structures, patterns, and relationships, automatically suggesting transformations and optimizations. For instance, AI algorithms can identify potential inconsistencies in data sources and recommend suitable data cleansing techniques.

2. Real-Time Data Transformation:

In the era of real-time analytics, the ability to transform data on the fly is gaining significance. Data transformation tools are evolving to handle streaming data and provide instant insights. For example, organizations can leverage real-time data transformation to process and analyze data from IoT devices as it's generated, enabling immediate decision-making and action.

3. Advanced Data Wrangling Techniques:

Data wrangling, which involves cleaning, structuring, and enriching data, will continue to advance. Future techniques will offer more sophisticated ways to handle complex data formats, unstructured data, and data with high dimensionality. Machine learning algorithms will play a role in automating data wrangling tasks, adapting to various data sources and structures.

4. Integration of Data Governance and Data Transformation:

Data governance will become an integral part of the data transformation process. Organizations will prioritize data quality, security, and compliance as they transform and integrate data from diverse sources. Automated data lineage tracking, metadata management, and data cataloging will ensure transparency and accountability in data transformation workflows.

5. Collaborative Data Transformation:

Data transformation will become a collaborative effort, involving data engineers, analysts, business users, and domain experts. Collaborative tools and platforms will allow different stakeholders to contribute to data transformation pipelines, ensuring that the final insights align with business goals.

6. Data Transformation as a Service:

Cloud-based services will offer data transformation capabilities as part of their offerings. Organizations can leverage these services to perform data transformation tasks without the need for extensive infrastructure setup. Data transformation as a service will facilitate scalability and cost-effectiveness, particularly for small and medium-sized businesses.

7. Ethical Data Transformation:

As data privacy and ethics gain prominence, data transformation practices will need to adhere to stricter ethical guidelines. Future trends will focus on ensuring that data transformation processes respect user privacy, comply with regulations, and avoid biases in data handling.

8. Continuous Data Transformation:

Data transformation will become an ongoing, iterative process rather than a one-time task. With data constantly evolving, organizations will implement continuous data transformation pipelines that adapt to changes in data sources, formats, and business requirements.

9. Interoperability and Standardization:

To facilitate seamless data transformation across different tools and platforms, the industry will move towards greater interoperability and standardization. This will enable data professionals to integrate diverse data sources and apply consistent transformation processes.

10. Augmented Data Transformation:

Augmented analytics will extend to data transformation, enhancing the capabilities of data professionals. AI-powered suggestions, auto-completion, and context-aware recommendations will streamline data transformation tasks, making the process more efficient and user-friendly.

Conclusion:

The landscape of data transformation is undergoing significant changes, driven by advancements in technology, analytics, and the increasing importance of data-driven decision-making. By staying informed about these future trends and embracing the evolving tools and techniques, data professionals can position themselves to harness the full potential of data transformation and drive innovation in their organizations. The journey ahead involves exploring new avenues, adopting cutting-edge tools, and embracing a mindset of continuous learning and adaptation to stay at the forefront of this dynamic field.

13.2. AI and Automation in Power Query

Artificial Intelligence (AI) and automation are rapidly transforming the landscape of data transformation, bringing unprecedented efficiency and accuracy to the process. This chapter delves into the integration of AI and automation within Power Query, a powerful tool in the realm of data transformation, and explores how these technologies are reshaping the way data professionals work.

1. Smart Data Profiling and Suggestion:

AI-driven automation in Power Query starts with intelligent data profiling. When connecting to a new data source, Power Query can automatically analyze the data and provide insights about its structure, quality, and potential issues. For instance, if there are missing values or inconsistent formats in a column, Power Query can suggest appropriate transformations to clean the data.

2. Auto-Generated Transformation Steps:

Power Query can harness AI to generate transformation steps based on the data's characteristics. For example, if you're dealing with a dataset containing date information, Power Query can automatically recognize it and offer transformation options like extracting year, quarter, or month. This streamlines the process and reduces manual intervention.

3. Natural Language Queries:

Future iterations of Power Query might include natural language processing capabilities. This would allow users to express their transformation requirements in plain English, and Power

KIET HUYNH

Query would interpret and execute the corresponding actions. For instance, you could type "summarize sales by category and month" and Power Query would generate the necessary code.

4. Smart Join and Merge Suggestions:

When combining multiple data sources, Power Query can utilize AI to suggest optimal join or merge operations based on data similarities, relationships, and patterns. This reduces the chances of errors and ensures more accurate data integration.

5. Intelligent Error Handling:

AI can enhance error handling by identifying potential issues in data transformation workflows. Power Query could provide real-time suggestions for resolving errors, such as suggesting a different data type conversion or proposing an alternative transformation step.

6. Automated Data Quality Checks:

AI-powered automation can continuously monitor data quality during transformations. If there's a sudden drop in data consistency or a spike in missing values, Power Query can trigger alerts or automatically apply corrective actions, ensuring that only high-quality data enters the pipeline.

7. Adaptive Query Execution:

As data sources and requirements evolve, Power Query could dynamically adjust transformation strategies. AI algorithms might analyze historical transformations and select the most efficient paths for data processing, improving performance over time.

8. Custom AI Models for Transformation:

Advanced users can leverage custom AI models within Power Query. For instance, you could train a machine learning model to categorize and transform specific data based on your business rules. This level of customization empowers organizations to tailor data transformations to their unique needs.

9. Automated Version Control and Documentation:

AI can assist in version control and documentation by tracking changes in data transformation steps and automatically generating documentation explaining each transformation. This ensures transparency, auditability, and easier collaboration among team members.

10. Predictive Transformation:

AI can predict future data transformation needs based on historical patterns and changing business requirements. Power Query might proactively suggest transformations to accommodate upcoming shifts in data sources or analytics goals.

Implementing AI and Automation in Power Query:

To harness the benefits of AI and automation in Power Query, follow these steps:

1. Stay Informed: Keep yourself updated about the latest AI advancements in data transformation and Power Query features.

2. Enable AI Features: Check for AI-powered features within Power Query. These might be available as updates or extensions.

3. Experiment: Start with small datasets and experiment with AI-driven suggestions and automation. Familiarize yourself with how Power Query uses AI to optimize transformations.

4. Leverage Documentation: Utilize resources provided by Power BI and Power Query documentation to learn about AI-driven capabilities and how to integrate them.

5. Customization: If applicable, explore creating custom AI models to tailor transformations to your specific needs.

6. Collaborate: Collaborate with other data professionals to share insights and best practices on using AI and automation effectively in Power Query.

Incorporating AI and automation into Power Query opens the door to a new era of data transformation. By leveraging these technologies, data professionals can streamline workflows, enhance accuracy, and drive more informed decision-making from the transformed data. As AI and automation continue to evolve, their integration into Power Query promises to reshape the landscape of data transformation in powerful and exciting ways.

13.3. The Road Ahead: Predictive Analytics and Beyond

The realm of data transformation is on the cusp of a significant evolution, propelled by the integration of predictive analytics and other innovative technologies. This section delves into the exciting future of data transformation, exploring the integration of predictive analytics and other emerging trends that are set to redefine how organizations process and analyze their data.

1. Predictive Analytics Redefining Data Transformation:

Predictive analytics is emerging as a transformative force in data transformation. Beyond merely cleansing and shaping data, predictive analytics empowers organizations to anticipate future trends and make proactive decisions. By combining historical data with machine learning algorithms, businesses can forecast outcomes and optimize data transformation processes to align with future needs.

2. Anticipating Transformation Needs:

Imagine a scenario where your data transformation tool uses predictive analytics to anticipate future data needs. Based on historical trends and changing business requirements, the tool could suggest upcoming transformations, saving time and effort. For example, if your sales data typically experiences a seasonal spike in the fourth quarter, the tool might proactively suggest creating quarterly aggregated tables to accommodate this trend.

3. Smart Data Sourcing and Integration:

Predictive analytics can revolutionize how data is sourced and integrated. By analyzing patterns, it can identify new potential data sources that could enrich your existing datasets. Moreover, it can offer insights on how to integrate these sources seamlessly, ensuring a comprehensive and accurate transformation process.

4. Enhanced Data Quality Control:

Predictive analytics can improve data quality control by flagging potential issues before they impact your analysis. It can predict data anomalies and inconsistencies, allowing you to address them during the transformation stage, resulting in more reliable and accurate insights.

5. Intelligent Transformation Workflows:

Imagine an intelligent data transformation platform that automatically adapts its workflows based on predictive insights. For instance, if the platform detects a sudden shift in customer behavior, it can automatically adjust transformation steps to accommodate this change, ensuring that your analysis remains up-to-date and relevant.

6. Integration of Augmented Reality (AR) and Virtual Reality (VR):

As technology advances, there's potential for data transformation to extend beyond traditional interfaces. AR and VR could be integrated to create immersive data transformation experiences. You might interact with your data in a virtual environment, allowing you to visually manipulate and shape it in real-time, enhancing your understanding and decision-making.

7. Blockchain-Enabled Data Transformation:

Blockchain's decentralized and tamper-resistant nature can revolutionize data transformation's security and traceability aspects. Imagine a future where every data transformation step is recorded on a blockchain, providing an immutable record of changes, approvals, and data lineage.

8. Conversational AI-Powered Data Transformation:

The integration of conversational AI, such as chatbots, can make data transformation more accessible to non-technical users. You could interact with a chatbot to express your transformation needs in natural language, and the AI would execute the necessary steps, making data transformation more user-friendly.

9. Continuous Learning Algorithms:

Data transformation tools could employ continuous learning algorithms to refine their transformation strategies over time. As they process new data and transformations, they learn from past experiences and adapt to changing trends, resulting in more optimized and efficient transformation processes.

10. The Human-AI Partnership:

The future of data transformation isn't solely about technology; it's about the collaboration between humans and AI. As AI handles more routine and predictive tasks, data professionals can focus on higher-level strategic thinking, drawing insights from predictive analytics to drive innovation and business growth.

Exploring Predictive Analytics and Beyond:

To embrace the future of data transformation, consider the following steps:

1. Stay Updated: Keep abreast of the latest developments in predictive analytics and emerging technologies.

2. Training and Upskilling: Invest in training to develop skills in predictive analytics, machine learning, and emerging technologies.

3. Adopt Pilot Projects: Implement pilot projects that integrate predictive analytics into your data transformation processes. Start small and gradually expand.

4. Collaborate: Engage with data science and AI experts to explore synergies between data transformation and predictive analytics.

5. Experiment with Emerging Technologies: As AR, VR, blockchain, and conversational AI evolve, experiment with their integration into your data transformation workflows.

6. Adapt and Evolve: Embrace a mindset of continuous improvement, adaptability, and openness to new technologies and methodologies.

The road ahead promises a transformative journey for data transformation. By harnessing the power of predictive analytics and emerging technologies, organizations can create more agile, insightful, and efficient data transformation processes, propelling them toward data-driven success in an ever-evolving digital landscape.

Appendix
Power Query Formula Reference

A.1 Common Power Query Functions and Syntax

In Power Query, functions play a crucial role in transforming and manipulating data. This appendix provides a comprehensive reference to common Power Query functions and their syntax, along with practical examples to illustrate their usage.

1. Text Functions:

a. Text.Length(text as nullable text) as number:

Returns the length of the input text.

Example:
```
```

let

   inputText = "Hello, Power Query!"

in

   Text.Length(inputText)
```
```

Output: 20

b. Text.Trim(text as nullable text) as text:

Removes leading and trailing spaces from the input text.

Example:

```
```

let

  inputText = "   Power Query   "

in

  Text.Trim(inputText)

```
```

Output: "Power Query"

2. Date and Time Functions:

a. Date.Year(date as date) as number:

Returns the year component of the input date.

Example:

```
```

let

  inputDate = #date(2023, 7, 15)

in

  Date.Year(inputDate)

```
```

Output: 2023

b. Date.MonthName(date as date, optional culture as nullable text) as text:

Returns the name of the month from the input date.

Example:

```
```
let

    inputDate = #date(2023, 7, 15)

in

    Date.MonthName(inputDate)
```
```

Output: "July"

3. Numeric Functions:

a. Number.Round(number as number, optional digits as nullable number) as number:

Rounds the input number to the specified number of decimal places.

Example:

```
```
let

    inputNumber = 15.6789

in

    Number.Round(inputNumber, 2)
```
```

```
```

Output: 15.68

b. Number.Abs(number as number) as number:

Returns the absolute value of the input number.

Example:

```
```

let

   inputNumber = -10

in

   Number.Abs(inputNumber)

```
```

Output: 10

4. List Functions:

a. List.Max(list as list) as any:

Returns the maximum value in the input list.

Example:

```
```

let

   inputList = {5, 10, 3, 8}

in

   List.Max(inputList)

```
```

Output: 10

b. List.Transform(list as list, transform as function) as list:

Applies the specified transformation function to each element in the input list.

Example:

```

let

   inputList = {1, 2, 3, 4},

   transformFunc = (x) => x * x

in

   List.Transform(inputList, transformFunc)

```
```

Output: {1, 4, 9, 16}

**5. Logical Functions:**

**a. Logical.And(expression1 as logical, expression2 as logical, ...) as logical:**

Returns TRUE if all input expressions are TRUE, otherwise returns FALSE.

Example:
```

```
```
let

    condition1 = true,

    condition2 = false

in

    Logical.And(condition1, condition2)
```
```

Output: false

b. Logical.Or(expression1 as logical, expression2 as logical, ...) as logical:

Returns TRUE if at least one input expression is TRUE, otherwise returns FALSE.

Example:

```
```
let

    condition1 = true,

    condition2 = false

in

    Logical.Or(condition1, condition2)
```
```

Output: true

This appendix provides just a glimpse of the wide range of functions available in Power Query. For a comprehensive list of functions and their syntax, refer to the official Power Query documentation. Experiment with these functions to create intricate data transformation steps tailored to your specific needs. By mastering the Power Query formula language, you can unlock the full potential of data transformation and analysis within Power BI.

A.2 Advanced Power Query Techniques

In this appendix, we delve into more advanced techniques within Power Query, exploring complex scenarios and showcasing powerful functions that can greatly enhance your data transformation process.

1. Custom Functions:

Creating custom functions allows you to encapsulate complex logic and reuse it across multiple queries. To define a custom function:

Step 1: Open the Power Query Editor.

Step 2: From the "Home" tab, click on "New Source" and select "Blank Query."

Step 3: In the formula bar, define your function using the `let` keyword.

Example: Creating a custom function to calculate the Fibonacci sequence.

```PowerQuery
let
    Fibonacci = (n) =>
        if n <= 1 then n
        else Fibonacci(n - 1) + Fibonacci(n - 2)
in
    Fibonacci
```

```
```
```

## 2. Error Handling and Custom Messages:

Dealing with errors gracefully is important in data transformation. Use the `try... otherwise` construct to handle errors and provide custom messages.

Example: Handling division by zero.

```PowerQuery
let
    div = (a, b) =>
        try a / b
        otherwise "Cannot divide by zero"
in
    div
```

3. Table.Group Function:

The `Table.Group` function lets you group data by one or more columns and apply aggregation to each group. This is useful for performing group-wise calculations.

Example: Grouping sales data by year and calculating total sales.

```PowerQuery
let
```
```

salesTable = ...

groupedTable = Table.Group(salesTable, {"Year"}, {{"Total Sales", each List.Sum([Sales]), type number}})

in

groupedTable

```

## 4. Recursive Queries:

Power Query supports recursion, which enables you to create iterative processes to transform data. Recursive queries are defined using the `let...in` construct.

Example: Calculating factorials using recursion.

```PowerQuery
let
    Factorial = (n) =>
        if n <= 1 then 1
        else n * Factorial(n - 1)
in
    Factorial
```

5. Advanced Join Techniques:
```

Power Query offers various join types beyond the basic inner and outer joins. You can perform anti-joins (exclude matching rows), left semi-joins (retain only left-side matching rows), and more.

Example: Performing an anti-join to find missing products.

```PowerQuery
let
    products = ...
    sales = ...
    missingProducts = Table.Join(products, "ProductID", sales, "ProductID", JoinKind.LeftAnti)
in
    missingProducts
```

6. Parameterized Queries:

Parameterizing queries enables dynamic filtering and customization of data extraction. You can create parameters in Power Query and reference them in your queries.

Example: Creating a parameter for the start date and filtering data based on it.

```PowerQuery
let
    startDate = #datetime(2023, 1, 1),
    sales = ...
    filteredSales = Table.SelectRows(sales, each [Date] >= startDate)
in
```

filteredSales

```
```

7. Advanced Data Type Conversions:

Power Query allows you to work with various data types, including records, tables, and lists. You can use functions like `Record.Field`, `Table.Column`, and `List.Distinct` to manipulate these data types.

Example: Extracting unique categories from a list of products.

```PowerQuery
let
    products = ...
    categories = List.Distinct(products[Category])
in
    categories
```

Mastering these advanced Power Query techniques will empower you to handle intricate data transformation scenarios with ease. Experiment and combine these techniques to build complex and insightful data transformations tailored to your specific requirements. The flexibility and power of Power Query make it an indispensable tool for data professionals seeking to extract meaningful   insights   from   their   data.

CONCLUSION

In the journey through "Power BI Data Transformation: From Data Source to Insights," we've embarked on a comprehensive exploration of the art and science of data transformation using Power Query. From the foundational principles to advanced techniques, this book has equipped you with the skills to effectively shape and manipulate your data, turning raw information into valuable insights.

Throughout the chapters, you've learned how to connect to diverse data sources, clean and prepare data, create complex transformations, model data effectively, and optimize performance. We've covered a range of real-world scenarios, providing you with practical examples, step-by-step instructions, and best practices that empower you to unleash the full potential of Power Query.

As you close this book, remember that data transformation is not just a technical process—it's a creative journey that allows you to sculpt your data into a meaningful story. The skills you've gained here will empower you to tackle the most intricate data challenges and uncover insights that drive informed decision-making.

A Heartfelt Thank You

We extend our sincere gratitude to you, our valued reader, for embarking on this educational journey with us. Your dedication to mastering data transformation is a testament to your commitment to excellence in the field of data analytics. We hope this book has served as a valuable resource, providing you with the knowledge and tools you need to transform data into actionable insights.

Your support and engagement mean the world to us. As you apply the skills you've acquired in your projects, experiments, and analyses, know that you're contributing to a world empowered by data-driven decisions.H

KIET HUYNH

If you have any feedback, questions, or insights to share, we're eager to hear from you. Please feel free to reach out through the provided contact information. We're here to support your ongoing journey in data transformation.

Thank you for choosing "Power BI Data Transformation: From Data Source to Insights." May your data transformation endeavors be rewarding and your insights transformative.